DEDICATION

What if you could sit and talk with Jesus? What if you could listen to Him tell you the story of His eternity in heaven, His miraculous birth, His life changing sermons, His miracles and His death and resurrection for you? Would your life be changed?

You would get closer to Jesus than ever before. You would love Him more and serve Him better. Your life would be transformed if you could talk to Jesus person to person.

Reading this book is like listening to Jesus talk to you. This book, *My Name is Jesus*, will change your life. It will do everything, that would happen to you if you could talk to Jesus.

Read and listen to Jesus tell you what is on His heart. Then pray and tell Jesus what is on your heart. Let Jesus touch you and in return you can touch him.

—The editors

My Name is
Jesus
Discover ME Through MY Names

My Name is JESUS

Copyright © 2018 Elmer L. Towns and Lee Fredrickson

Published by Destiny Image
Shippensburg, PA 17257
and
21st Century Press
Springfield, MO 65807

Bible images from The Life of Jesus used by permission
© By Intellectual Reserve, Inc.

Destiny Image and 21st Century Press are Christian publishers dedicated to publishing books that have a high standard of family values. We believe the vision for our companies is to provide families and individuals with user-friendly materials that will help them in their daily lives and experiences. It is our prayer that this book will help you discover Biblical truth for your own life and help you meet the needs of others. May God richly bless you.

ISBN TP: 978-0-7684-4538-1
ISBN eBook: 978-0-7684-4539-8
ISBN Large Print: 978-0-7684-4540-4
ISBN Hard Cover: 978-7684-4541-1

Cover and Book Design: Lee Fredrickson

Visit our website at: www.destinyimage.com
Printed in the United States of America

CONTENTS

Dedication 3

Introduction...7

PART ONE

1. My Name is Jesus 11
2. My Title is "Lord" 19
3. My Office Title is "Christ" 27

PART TWO

4. My Old Testament Prophetic Names.................................41
5. My Salvational Names 49
6. My Birth Names 57
7. My Service Names 71
8. My Sonship Names 81
9. My Godhead Names 89
10. My Jehovistic Titles 97
11. My Church Names 107
12. My Apocalyptic Names 113

APPENDIX

My Names and Titles In Scripture.................................125

My Preeminent Pronouns in scripture 144

Compound Names of The Lord God (Jehovah El) in Scripture....146

Names of God (Elohim) in Scripture.................................146

Names of Jehovah in Scripture 148

A Selected Bibliography of My Names 149

INTRODUCTION

Hello . . . My name is Jesus. There are many ways to learn about Me. You can study how I lived, or My miracles, or My sermons, or the way I talk to people. You can see My full deity in the things I said, and you can also see my full humanity in the gospels.

But I want to tell you about all My names, offices, titles, and pictures of Me in scripture. Each one gives a glimpse of who I am and what I do. When you put all of them together, you begin to grasp who I, the Son of God, am.

Why are there so many names about Me? Because I am God. My many names reflect My many qualities, even then there are many things about Me you will never know. Remember, as God I am eternal . . . omniscient . . . omnipresent . . . and omnipotent. These are qualities that humans can't comprehend . . . measure . . . or fully understand.

You can never completely know Me because you don't have a divine mind to know all things. Only the Father and the Holy Spirit know Me completely and understand every aspect of My life.

There are over 700 names-references to Me in scripture. Some of these are names I gave Myself, some are names given to Me by the Father, or the Holy Spirit. Other names are given to Me by humans who spoke under divine inspiration and/or direction by the Father or Holy Spirit. They spoke so people would know things about Me that were previously unknown.

And then, some of My names-references were given to Me by humans as they reacted to Me. What they said about Me was an honest response of a time, and so these names were included in scripture. You might have had the same true response if you met Me in the same way.

Gloria Gaither once wrote a song about Me and said, "There's something about that name . . . ." I love this song because people have used it in worship and/or praise. Of course she was referring to My name *Jesus*. And I appreciate the fact that she has endeared My name—Jesus—to so many followers.

Let's come back to the original question, "Why do I have so many names-references?" There are several answers to that question. First, no one name can fully describe who I am, and even if you look at all My names used in scripture, you still won't completely know Me. But learn My many names to know Me better or more intimately.

Second, perhaps I have so many names because there are many facets of My personality or nature. I am love . . . holiness . . . justice . . . truth . . . goodness . . . and I am a friend that sticks closer than a brother.

A third reason why I have so many names is because I do so many things. It takes a vast number of names-references to tell all I can do. For instance, I am your Savior, your King . . . your Guide . . . your Intercessor . . . and the One who indwells you.

A fourth reason has to do with time of need. Sometimes My many names would overwhelm you and you wouldn't know what to call Me. You'd be searching for the appropriate name to call Me and not know which one to use. So come to Me with your needs. Just come in prayer . . . because you hurt . . . because you're thankful . . . or you need something desperately . . . right away. In that instant you may not use the right name. Use any name . . . you'll probably use a name that's close to your need.

Once Elmer Towns drove out of a fog on Highway 80 in Louisiana, and smashed into a milk truck at full speed. He crumpled to the floor board of that car; his head was bleeding. When he regained consciousness he cried out to Me, "Shepherd . . . Lord, I need You. You are my Shepherd; I need you *now*." Then he prayed the 23rd Psalm on that floor board and in the ambulance on the way to the hospital. It was a terrible scene and yes, he needed Me, but everything is fine now. If you look carefully you will see that scar in his forehead that reminds him of the accident.

I have one name that you'll never know. When heaven opens and I return in the Second Coming on a white horse into the Battle of Armageddon, I have attached to My clothing, "A name that no one knows" (Rev. 19:14). The Father knows it and so does the Holy Spirit. Only We know what it means. But you can't know it simply because you're human and there are things about Deity you can never understand because you have a finite mind.

This book is written so you can study over 700 of My names-references so you can know Me better. Remember Paul cried out, "That

I may know Him . . ." (Phil. 3:10). It's not just head knowledge he wanted. He wanted to know My heart, My passion . . . he wanted to know Me as a person. Not know about one, but to know Me personally. Read the New Testament the accounts how I used Paul, he opened up nations to the gospel, he took the gospel where it had never gone. He built powerful churches, won multitudes to salvation, and suffered many things for Me. He was beaten . . . starved . . . robbed . . . stoned to death . . . and finally he died as a martyr.

Because Paul knew me perhaps more than any other human, he was able to do more than any other human. That is my challenge to you. Know Me.

Study these 700 name-references to learn all you can in your head, but let it seep down into your heart until you can feel deep love for Me. Then let it seep even deeper into your will so that you are committed to making Me first in everything you are and do.

The more you learn about Me, and the more you know what I can do for you, the richer your life will become. You will grow and be able to move mountain-barriers. And talking to Me in prayer, you can reach out and touch Me as never before. Then I will reach back to touch you in an incredible way.

—Jesus

PART ONE

My Name, the
Lord Jesus Christ

CHAPTER ONE

MY NAME IS JESUS

"And she will bring forth a Son, and you shall call His name Jesus,
for He will save His people from their sins" (Matthew 1:21)

There are more than 700 of My names and titles in Scripture. None is perhaps more venerated by Christians than My name "Jesus." A contemporary songwriter acknowledges simply, "There's just something about that name." The very sound of My name is precious in the ears of Christians worldwide. My name has brought about a sense of overwhelming comfort to many in their darkest hours. Jesus is My name most often verbalized in prayer and preaching, in testimony and witnessing. Many relate dramatic, even miraculous experiences of life to the significance of My name.

My name "Jesus" was, at the time of My earthly sojourn, among the most popular of names selected by parents of Hebrew boys. In the writings of the Jewish historian Josephus, at least twenty different men, ten of whom were My contemporaries also had My name Jesus. Its popularity was probably to a large extent due to its relationship with one of Israel's great leaders, Joshua, the son of Nun and successor to Moses. In the Egyptian papyri, the name occurs frequently right through the early part of the second century. Then abruptly, both Jews and Christians stopped using "Jesus" as a name for their baby boys. The Jews did so because it was so closely related to Christianity, which they rigorously opposed and hated. The Christians refused to use the name for opposite reasons. To them, the name was special and held in veneration. It was almost thought sacrilegious that anyone but Me should bear that name.

When you read the New Testament, you will be impressed with how often My name appears. My name Jesus is by far the most often used name in the Gospels; and, even in the book of Acts, where you see My title "Lord" often used, the use of "Jesus" outnumbers "Lord" three to one. In the Epistles, My name Jesus continues to occur, though not as often. It formed an intrinsic part of the great Pauline formula by which the apostle often referred to "The Lord, Jesus Christ," i.e., "Lord" (My Title), "Jesus" (My Name), and "Christ" (My Office).

What is perhaps most surprising about My name "Jesus" is not its use but the absence of its use. With the possible exception of the thief on the cross (Luke 23:42), there is no record of anyone ever addressing Me directly by My name "Jesus" during My earthly life and ministry. Further, I apparently used this name to identify Myself only twice, both occasions to persons after My ascension to and glorification in heaven (cf. Acts 9:5; Revelation 22:16).

THE MEANING OF MY IDENTIFICATION

When Mary and Joseph talked to Me, their son, they used their native language and called Me "Yeshua" or "Joshua." When they used the Greek trade language, then they called Me "Jesus," as noted previously, "Jesus" is the Greek form of the Hebrew name "Joshua." The name "Joshua" was a contraction of "Jehoshua," meaning "Jehovah the Savior." It was used to identify several men in the Old Testament, the best known being Joshua the son of Nun, who led Israel into the land of Canaan. Actually, Joshua's given name was "Hoshea," meaning "salvation," and was changed to "Jehoshua" or "Joshua" by Moses, probably when he sent him to spy out the land at Kadesh-barnea (Numbers 13:16).

My name "Jesus/Joshua" is built on the Hebrew verb stem *yasha* meaning "saved." The first use of this verb in Scripture is also the embryonic first mention of the doctrine of salvation (Exodus 14:30). The salvation of Israel is defined in terms of the destruction of the army of Egypt in the Red Sea. This miracle, so often referred to in the Old Testament, is also a type of the salvation from sin I provided on the cross.

As borne by Joshua, the name was an expression of faith in what My Father could and would do for Our people and a testimony to the effect that I, Jesus, was willing to be a part of it. No doubt a major aspect of that salvation was viewed in a military light as the nation went out to destroy the inhabitants of the land and settle it as their own.

Still, the spiritual salvation of the nation and its families, individually or corporately, was not overlooked.

Several Bible commentators have noted the typical significance of Joshua which goes far beyond a mere similarity of names. Joshua was the shadow of what I am in reality. This is particularly true in My name. When I was so named by the angel, it was more than simply an expression of the Messianic hope of Israel. It was an affirmation of My real identity and primary concern. "Jesus" means "Jehovah the Savior," but when applied to Me, it is a declaration that I am *Jehovah the Savior*. It both enshrines and expresses the mystery of My Person and the marvels of My work.

THE MYSTERY OF MY INCARNATION

In the first mentions of My name Jesus in Scripture, it is clear that I was more than just another baby boy born to a young Jewish mother. The first to hear My name was Mary who was informed not only that she would bear a son but that she should "call My name JESUS" and that I would also "be called the Son of the Highest" (Luke 1:31,32). When Joseph first heard the name, he was told "that which is conceived in her is of the Holy Ghost" (Matthew 1:20). The name "Jesus," when applied to Me the virgin-born child of Bethlehem, was an affirmation of who I am, "Jehovah the Savior."

"Jehovah" was the most venerated name of the Godhead in the Old Testament. So careful were the Jews not to violate the fourth commandment that they refused to verbalize this name lest, unknowingly, they used it in vain. When they came to read it in their Scriptures, by habit they substituted the name *Adonai*, another name for the Godhead in the Old Testament. Because the Hebrew language lacks vowels, words are pronounced as they are learned. But when the pious Jews refused to pronounce My name "Jehovah," people were soon unsure as to the actual pronunciation of it. Most applied the vowels of *Adonai* to it and pronounce the name "Jehovah." More critical scholars have chosen to pronounce My name "Yahweh." Actually, because accents and dialects of a language change as that language is used over the years, it is impossible to be certain how Moses first pronounced this name when he introduced it to Israel.

That greatly respected name "Jehovah" of the Old Testament was actually Me in the New Testament! I Jehovah became a man. That mystery concerning the incarnation has baffled theologians and Bible students for years, yet it remains a part of human history that one day, I who made this world and created all things, including the human race, voluntarily chose to become a man without compromising who I was. No wonder My name has such a special significance for Christians. Certainly, if the unsaved Jews were so concerned about using Jehovah's name in vain that they avoided any possibility of doing so, Christians today ought also to reverence and respect My name Jehovah incarnate, *Jesus*, and never use it in vain as a curse.

When you realize My true nature, you have no problem understanding the necessity of the virgin birth. It is not simply an early Christian legend which found its way into the Bible or a novel little miracle to give you yet something else to believe. The virgin birth was the only possible way in which I—Jehovah—could become a man and at the same time remain Jehovah. I needed a human mother to have a human nature. If I had had a human father, I also would have received the sin nature of My father. With a pair of sinful human parents, it would have been impossible for Me to be the Son of God. So I was born without the help of a human father so I would be sinless and remain God.

When I created man, I made man holy—that is, without sin. But man's holiness was conditional and ended when Adam fell into sin. Since then, men have been born sinners by nature because they inherited their nature from their father, Adam. "Wherefore, as by one man sin entered into the world, and death by sin; and so death passed upon all men, for that all have sinned" (Romans 5:12). That would also have been My fate had I been the physical son of Joseph. In contrast, the Scriptures teach that I knew no sin (II Corinthians 5:21), was without sin (Hebrews 4:15), and did no sin (I Peter 2:22).

THE MARVELS OF MY OCCUPATION

When Joseph learned his legal son would be named "Jesus," he was also told the nature of My work, "For he shall save his people from their sins" (Matthew 1:21). I was not only salvation, but would also provide salvation for My people. The full nature or extent of that salvation may not have been fully understood at first. Initially, it was widely believed that the salvation provided by Me was exclusively for the Jews. This view is evident even in the book of Acts, where Peter is reluctant to go to Cornelius' household and later where the Jerusalem Conference becomes a necessity.

Surprisingly, it was the Samaritans who first recognized the broader extent of My salvation that I would affect. Their understanding of "the Christ, the Savior of the world" (John 4:42), was unheard of in Jewish circles and largely ignored in the early days of the church. You might argue that the extent of My work was never fully realized in practice even by the church until the Jerusalem Conference (Acts 15).

THE MAJESTY OF MY REPUTATION

A name is a reputation. Sometimes one gains a reputation from a name, and at other times a person gives his name a reputation. When Elmer Towns was growing up in Savannah, Georgia, his mother would frequently remind him to live up to their family name. "Remember, you're a Towns." Their family history went back several generations in Georgia and included several prominent medical doctors, one of whom served for a time as governor of the state. As children, Elmer, his brother, and sister, were encouraged to live up to the historical reputation of their name.

Just as Elmer's mother reminded him to live up to the reputation of his family name, all Christians need to be reminded to live up to the reputation of My name, Jesus. The Apostle Paul reminded the Jews in Rome that "the name of God is blasphemed among the Gentiles through you" as a result of their inconsistent living (Romans 2:23,24). The same could be said of Christians today. When you behave in a manner inconsistent with My name Jesus, the unsaved world takes note of your hypocrisy and lowers its estimate of Me and Christianity. How many Christians have been reminded of "hypocrites in the church" as they have tried to win their unsaved friends, relatives, associates, and neighbors?

Many Christians today conclude their prayers with the phrase, "in Jesus' name." Sometimes they will cite John 14:13,14 or 16:23 as biblical authority for that practice. In those texts I encouraged My disciples to "ask in My name." Actually, to ask in My name means to ask in My Person and does not mean that every prayer must end with the words "in Jesus' name." Some who pray this way do so wrongly, viewing the mention of My name as a kind of magical incantation that will guarantee an answer to their prayers. Others use the expression as a constant reminder that when they pray, they do so on My merits and not of themselves.

There is a certain power in My name, however, that transcends your ability to understand it fully. It is a power over demons themselves. Even the Jewish exorcists of the first century recognized this spiritual power and sought to harness it by addressing and commanding demons in My name (Acts 19:13). The failure of the sons of Sceva to overcome the demons on that occasion emphasized the fact that the power of My name is not in the mere recital of a formula but power is in Me, a person. The sons of Sceva did not have a personal relationship with Me and, therefore, could not effectively use My name in order to cast out demons.

I encouraged My disciples to ask for "anything" in My name (John 14:14), including the salvation of unsaved friends, relatives, associates and neighbors, or solutions to problems in your family or finances. My name—Jesus—is the "name which is above every name" (Philippians 2:9). My name Jesus is powerful to save from hell, and powerful to keep those who are saved. I alone am powerful enough both to control demons and influence God the Father. You should speak, sing, meditate, and glory in My name—Jesus. It is even proper to fall in adoration and worship at My name Jesus (Philippians 2:10).

CONCLUSION

Have you ever noticed how many of your favorite hymns make specific reference to My name—Jesus? Leaf through the average church hymnal, and you will agree that My name has certainly inspired its share of songs. Many of the most familiar hymns referring to Me use the name "Jesus." And this is not only a phenomenon among English-speaking Christians. Though pronounced differently in other parts of the world, My name "Jesus" has found a prominent place in the expressions of biblical Christianity, regardless of the linguistic or cultural background of the Christian. My name is constantly sung and preached by those who have come to love Me. They love Me because I first loved them and demonstrated My love from a cross.

Is it any wonder My name—Jesus—is so deeply loved by Christians around the world? It is the name that brings salvation and provides all the assistance you need in facing the struggles of life. My name bears witness to the fact that I, Jehovah the Savior, became a man at one point in history so you might spend eternity with Me in heaven. My challenge to you is to come with boldness to the throne of grace in prayer, knowing before you pray that I am there to give you grace even before you recognize your need. The songwriter was right: "There is something about My name"!

For Discussion:

1. What does My name Jesus mean? Why was it popular when Joseph and Mary gave it to their Son?
2. Why did parents discontinue naming their sons Jesus? What does this teach you about your attitude toward My name Jesus?
3. What does it mean to "live up to My name Jesus"?
4. Should you end your prayers by saying "in Jesus' name"? Why or why not?
5. Name your favorite hymn about Me. Why is it your favorite hymn?

CHAPTER TWO

MY TITLE IS "LORD"

"For there is born to you this day in the city of David a Savior, who is Christ the Lord (Luke 2:11).

"Therefore let all the house of Israel know assuredly that God has made this Jesus, whom you crucified, both Lord and Christ" (Acts 2:36).

"That if you confess with your mouth the Lord Jesus and believe in your heart that God has raised Him from the dead, you will be saved" (Romans 10:9).

People change their names as their role in life and office changes. When Elmer Towns began teaching, his students called him "Prof. Towns." Later, after receiving his first doctorate, they called him "Dr. Towns." As dean of the B. R. Lakin School of Religion, he is sometimes referred to as "Dean Towns." Changing titles marked changes in his life.

When his children began having children of their own, Towns thought he was too young to be a grandfather! He told his children not to teach his grandchildren to call him Grandfather, or some cute name like "Poppa. " His daughter, not wanting to offend, taught her daughter to address him as "Dr. Towns." For a while it worked, but the child soon learned that this man was really "Poppa." Also, this little girl noticed that her father often called his father-in-law "Doc." Soon she began addressing him as "Poppa Doc." Although the title was once that of a Haitian dictator, he is now more than pleased to be called "Poppa Doc" by his grandchildren.

Similarly, My name has changed over the years as My role and office have changed. In the Gospels, I am most often called "Jesus," although both My title "Lord" and office "Christ" were emphasized at My birth (Luke 2:11). It was not until the book of Acts that the title "Lord" became more commonly used and began to take on the characteristics of that name. When Luke was writing the early history of the church, he chose "Lord" as My narrative name. Probably "Jesus" was considered too familiar to be used and, "Christ" at that time sounded too formal. Another advantage of this title is that it conveyed the idea of relationship. If I Jesus am Lord, I am Lord of something or someone.

I am Jesus the Lord of your life whether you let Me operate in your life or not. I am by My nature the Lord. Ultimately a lord has dominion over someone. I, the Lord, want to be your Lord. If you do not recognize Me as Lord now, someday you will call Me Lord when every tongue will confess that I, Jesus Christ, am Lord (Philippians 2:11). You may choose to recognize Me as Lord today or be forced to recognize Me as Lord at My return to earth.

The normal posture of kneeling in prayer traditionally practiced by Christians is a symbolic recognition of My lordship. As you pray, it is common for you to bow your head. That is the usual way of approaching the monarch or supreme ruler of a region. That is the way in which you will approach Me as King of kings and Lord of lords. When you bow, you are symbolically showing your allegiance to Me.

THE MEANING OF MY NAME LORD

In calling Me "Lord," a speaker could have been using that term in one of several ways. The Greek word *kurios* is used in the New Testament with reference to an owner (Luke 19:33), one who has disposal of anything (Matthew 12:8), a master to whom service is due (Matthew 6:24), an emperor or king (Acts 25:26; Revelation 17:14), a title of respect for a father (Matthew 21:30), husband (I Peter 3:6), master (Matthew 13:27), ruler (Matthew 27:63), angel (Acts 10:4), a stranger (Acts 16:30), a designation of a pagan idol or deity (I Corinthians 8:5), as well as a translation of the name of God from the Old Testament: (*Jehovah*, Matthew 4:7; *Adonai*, Matthew 1:22, and *Elohim*, I Peter 1:25). There is no Bible reference that Christians used this term for anyone but Me, suggesting it was used as a recognition of My deity.

The translation of Hebrew titles *Jehovah, Adonai,* and *Elohim* by the Greek word *kurios* (Lord) emphasizes that My titles in the Old Testament are also to be included in My name Jesus. The use of the word *kurios* in this way recognizes that several rights belong to Me. First, there is the right to respect. This word Lord was commonly used as an address of respect, not only to those in authority, such as kings and fathers, but even to strangers. Secondly, there is the right to be served. When one used the title "Lord," it normally expressed a willingness to serve a person. A third implied right is disposal. An owner, or lord, could dispose of his property in any way he saw fit. This is an important concept to remember in the area of our stewardship of My resources. Finally, the right to rule and hold authority over others is also implied in the name "lord."

In the cultural context of that day, a lord had absolute authority over his subjects. When I was called "Lord" by Christians, they used that word as a title of My deity.

The use of Lord was significant in the lives and experience of the disciples. When I told Peter to let down his nets, Peter respectfully addressed Me as "Master" and let down a net (Luke 5:5). He let down only one net suggesting he was doing so merely as a courtesy to Me and did not expect to catch anything. Later, when the net broke because of the size of the catch, Peter realized I was more than just another religious teacher; then he addressed Me as "Lord" (Luke 5:8).

At the last supper, the speech of the disciples revealed the nature of their faith and true attitude toward Me. When I announced that one of the twelve would betray Me that night, the eleven asked, "Lord, is it I" (Matthew 26:22). Later, Judas also answered but said, "Master, is it I?" (Matthew 26:25). The eleven disciples had come to recognize Me as Lord, but for Judas, I was only a boss or master.

The third significant use of this title by a disciple is the time when Thomas called Me Lord. I had invited him to touch My wounds with his fingers and hands. But he cried out, "My Lord and my God" (John 20:28). His affirmation of faith in Me as *Jehovah El* of the Old Testament is the apex of the Gospel of John and the highest statement of deity attributed to Me up until that time. John writes his Gospel in such a way as to build to a climax with Thomas' affirmation of My Lordship. This expression of faith by Thomas is hopefully yours too.

21

"Lord" is the most often used of My names in the book of Acts. It was the name the Father used of Me at the resurrection (Philippians 2:9-11). My lordship is a post-resurrection emphasis. It is a constant theme in apostolic preaching. "For we preach not ourselves, but Christ Jesus the Lord; and ourselves your servants for Jesus' sake" (II Corinthians 4:5).

THE MESSAGE OF MY NAME

As is true with each of My names in Scripture, My name "Lord" has a special significance in the life of every Christian. It closely relates to what it means to be a Christian. "That if thou shalt confess Me with your mouth—the Lord Jesus—and shalt believe in your heart that the Father hath raised Me from the dead, you shalt be saved" (Romans 10:9). Some evangelists erroneously argue that this means a person is not saved if his conversion is not accompanied by a dramatic evidence of repentance. Although repentance is as important as faith in conversion, the *evidence* of repentance differs in every experience.

If My name, Lord, has convicted an unsaved person about a particular sin and he refuses to repent of that sin, he cannot be saved until he is willing to recognize Me as Lord in that area of his life. Often, however, it is not until after a person is saved that he is convicted by the Holy Spirit of sin in his life. This presence of sin does not mean that I am not your Savior, only that I am not recognized as your Lord.

Recognizing "My Lordship" is a work of the Holy Spirit in your life. "No man can say that I am the Lord, but by the Holy Ghost" (I Corinthians 12:3). All Christians at some point in their walk with deity need to put Me on the throne of their life as Lord. "But sanctify Me the Lord God in your hearts," the Apostle Peter urged (I Peter 3:15). Paul urged essentially the same things of the Romans when he said, "I beseech you therefore, brethren, by the mercies of the Father, that ye present your bodies a living sacrifice, holy, acceptable unto Me, which is your reasonable service" (Romans 12:1).

Lordship is the foundation of practicing biblical stewardship. Stewardship is not just fund raising; it is also managing your life. It is placing your all on the altar for Me. Stewardship is recognizing not just the tithe as Mine—that is, ten percent—but that all of your money is Mine. All that you have is Mine. "The earth is Mine, and the fullness thereof; the world, and they who dwell therein" (Psalm 24:1). I am Lord both by creation, redemption, and stewardship.

Lordship is an experience for the believer rather than the unsaved. What is today referred to as "Lordship Salvation" is almost a statement of salvation by works, but the Scriptures teach that you are saved solely by grace. Lordship is for the Christian; grace is for the unsaved. Failure to recognize Me as Lord in your life will result in frustration in your Christian experience. If you never yield control of your life to Me, you will constantly have doubts concerning the certainty of your salvation.

Lordship marks the progress or growth of your Christian life as you confess and forsake known sin in the process of becoming more like Me. George Mueller grew in grace as a Christian. On several occasions God revealed areas in his life to be corrected. As Mueller confessed his sin and surrendered that area of his life to My lordship, he continued to grow in Me.

Lordship means surrender. In a meeting of several well-known Christian workers in the last century, the question was asked what was the greatest need in Christian circles at that time. Without hesitation, a Scottish missionary leader summed up that need in two words, "absolute surrender." He went on to explain that most of the problems he dealt with in his ministry would resolve themselves if Christians would surrender themselves totally and absolutely to My lordship. Many Christian leaders today would agree that this is still the greatest need of the church.

I said, "If any man will come after me, let him deny himself, and take up his cross daily, and follow me" (Luke 9:23). The key to the victorious Christian life is found in surrendering or yielding oneself wholeheartedly to Me. "Neither yield ye your members as instruments of unrighteousness unto sin: but yield yourselves unto Me, as those that are alive from the dead, and your members as instruments of righteousness unto God" (Romans 6:13).

Paul uses four key verbs in Romans 6 which describe various aspects of what it means to call Me "Lord." These are keys to the victorious Christian life. The first verb is "know" (6:3,6,9). You must first know the doctrinal basis of victory in the Christian life—that is, that you are united to and identified with Me in My death and resurrection. The next verb is "reckon" (6:11), which means to count or rely upon these facts to be true concerning yourselves. The verb "yield" (6:13,16,19) means to present yourselves once and for all to Me as My possession and for My use. The fourth verb, "obey" (6:16,17), urges you to be continuously obedient to the revealed and known will of God the Father.

Lordship is more than just yielding; lordship means control. An overemphasis on yielding sometimes results in passive Christians. But I want more than yielded Christians; I want control of your life. When I have control, you will take up your cross. When I have control, you will deny yourself and the flesh. When I have control, you will find yourselves saying no to your "old man" and yes to your "new man." When I have control, you will prepare, do your best, and work as hard as you can to serve the heavenly Father.

When I taught the parable of the talents, I emphasized several principles of lordship or biblical stewardship. One of the most significant is that the Father expects production from what He has given you to use. Don't take My resources, which I have entrusted to your keeping, and hoard them or bury them in the ground. That is the greatest disobedience you can do toward Me. When I entrust you with My resources, I expect you to use them and multiply them.

CONCLUSION

Recognizing My lordship should be the norm in the Christian's life. I taught a parable concerning the duty of the servant was constantly to obey his master and concluded with the words, "So likewise you, when you shall have done all those things which are commanded you, say, We are unprofitable servants: we have done that which was our duty to do" (Luke 17:10). The concept of a Christian who does not recognize My lordship in his life is foreign to the New Testament ideal.

Yet, such Christians are all too common today. The greatest need of the church is still absolute surrender. Someday, of course, "at My name every knee should bow, of things in heaven, and things in earth, and things under the earth: and that every tongue should confess that I am Lord, to the glory of God the Father" (Philippians 2:10,11). When it comes to recognizing My lordship, you have a choice. It can be your decision now, or Mine later.

For Discussion:

1. What did the word Lord mean in the culture when I lived physically on earth?
2. Explain the term "My Lordship."
3. Can you recall a time when you surrendered your life to Me your Lord? (Be ready to share briefly.)
4. Explain the statement: "I am the Lord of your life whether you let Me operate in your life or not."
5. Where will you be when "everyone" recognizes My Lordship?

CHAPTER THREE

MY OFFICE TITLE IS "CHRIST"

"Come, see a man, which told me all things that ever I did: is not this the Christ?" (John 4:29).

At least forty-nine times in his Epistles, Paul uses the expression "the/our Lord Jesus Christ," bringing together My three primary names. As noted, "Lord" is My title, "Jesus" is My name, and "Christ" is My office. Actually, "Christ" is a favorite name of the Apostle Paul, and he uses it independently of other titles some 211 times in his writings. In addition, he often uses this title with My other names and titles. For Paul, the title "Christ" had a very special significance.

The Greek word *Christos*, translated "Christ," literally means "anointed one" and was used in the Septuagint to translate the word "Messiah" (cf. Daniel 9:25,26). The Messiah in the Old Testament is the word Christ in the New Testament. They refer to the same Person, although their contextual use affects their perspective somewhat. In the Old Testament, "Messiah" is always used in the context of a Messianic hope, whereas the predominate use of "Christ" in the New Testament is as an official name of Jesus in the context of My work completed.

Theologians speak of My three anointed offices, meaning Me as *prophet, priest,* and *king*. This expression seems to have been first used by Eusebius in the third century to explain the biblical teaching concerning My office. Even though the writers of Scripture did not express it in so many words, the fact that I was viewed by them in the context of the Old Testament anointed offices is particularly evident in the book of Revelation. The title of the book implies the nature of My *prophetic* office in revealing or making known what was otherwise hidden (Revelation 1:1).

In John's first vision of Me (1:13), I am viewed wearing a *talar*, a technical word referring to the robe of the *priest*. The office of *king* is seen in Revelation 11:15, where the theme of the book may be summarized: "And the seventh angel sounded; and there were great voices in heaven, saying, The kingdoms of this world are become the kingdoms of our Lord, and of his Christ, and he shall reign forever and ever." This theme is developed throughout the book until I am pictured as returning and having "on his vesture and on his thigh a name written, KING OF KINGS, AND LORD OF LORDS" (19:16).

Although the Old Testament context is important in understanding the implications of the name "Christ," you must again remember that I not only took the reputation of a name upon Myself but also added something of My reputation to the name. This is certainly evident as you see how the Apostle Paul gave the title "Christ" greater clarity in his writings. Paul ministered mostly among Gentiles, to whom the title "Christ" would be meaningless without the Old Testament background. In his various epistles he gave the title "Christ" a fuller meaning for such readers, particularly in the context of My union and communion with the believer. In many respects, therefore, the apostle must be credited with transforming My office into a personal name–Christ—for the One who was the Messiah and much more.

When a young man graduates from medical school and moves to a small town to begin private practice, the members of the community might use the title "Doctor" with great respect as a prefix to his name. But as the years pass and the doctor becomes more and more a part of the community, the title "Doctor" often becomes the nickname "Doc." Similarly, Paul took the title "Messiah" and made it My personal name by which many Christians today refer to Me. Many people refer to Me as Christ, rather than calling Me Jesus.

MESSIAH IN THE OLD TESTAMENT

Throughout the pages of Old Testament, the prophets of Israel and Judah displayed a pervasive Messianic hope. In their messages, which were often characterized by coming doom, often there was also a distant hope that ultimate deliverance would come from God.

This deliverance was more than a supernatural phenomenon; it was the work of an anointed servant of God designated "the Messiah" (cf. Daniel 9:25). This title, which became My name, was a title of My preincarnation in that eternal day before the beginning of time. From the very beginning, opposition to God is the same as opposition to Me, called "his anointed" (Psalm 2:2). In the consummation of this age, the kingdom of Jehovah is identical to the kingdom "of his Christ" (Revelation 11:15).

In the context of the Old Testament, the term "Messiah" or "Anointed One" had specific relevance to the three offices of Prophet, Priest and King. A candidate was normally initiated or inducted into his office by an act of anointing—the offices of Prophet, Priest, and King. Because of this it has been called the "Threefold Anointed Office."

Prophetically, the coming Messiah ("anointed one") was portrayed as holding each of the offices. Typically, the New Testament identifies Me with the Prophet Moses (cf. Deuteronomy 18:15-19), the Priest Melchizedek (cf. Psalm 110:4), and King David (II Samuel 7:12,13). The candidate for each of these offices was anointed with oil to begin ministry in the office (cf. I Kings 19:16; Exodus 29:6,7; I Samuel 16:13). In fulfillment of the type, I was anointed by the Holy Spirit as I began My public ministry (Matthew 3:16; Mark 1:10,11; Luke 3:21,22; John 1:32,33).

You must assume that the early disciples understood the title "Christ" in the Old Testament context of "the Messiah." John the Baptist confessed that he, himself, was not I (John 1:20), yet those who left John to follow Me announced boldly, "We have found the Messiah" (John 1:41).

My divine anointing for ministry was important in both My teaching and in the Jerusalem church (cf. Luke 4:18; Acts 10:38). From the very beginning, the early church understood Me in terms of My Threefold Anointed Office—Prophet, Priest, and King.

I Am the Anointed Prophet

Few people would deny My prophetic ministry even if they might reject the content of My teaching. It is a common practice among those who deny My deity and the unique redemptive nature of My work, at least to acknowledge Me as a moral teacher and religious prophet. Of course, My prophetic office as revealed in Scripture was far more specific than the vague description Me as a prophet by a liberal teacher.

There are five designations which identify the prophet in the Old Testament. First, he was called "the man of God" (Deuteronomy 33: 1; I Samuel 2:27; 9:6; I Kings 13: 1; Psalm 90:title). This expression relates particularly to My unique relationship to the Father and the uniqueness of My message. It also assumed that the prophet had a godly character.

The second title of the prophet was the "servant of God" (II Kings 17:13,23; 21:10; 24:2; Ezra 9:11; Jeremiah 7:25). Although no prophet ever called himself My servant, I often referred to the prophets as My servants. Some commentators think this might be part of the reason the writers of the New Testament so often began their epistles with such expressions as "servant of God" or "the servant of the Lord Jesus Christ." Also, inasmuch as it was customary for a Jew to begin his prayer to the Father by identifying himself as His servant; we may assume that this title, when applied to the prophets, referred to them as men of prayer. The predominant feature of this designation is that of the Master/slave relationship that existed between Me and My servants, the prophets.

A third and by far most common designation of the prophet in the Old Testament was the Hebrew word *nabi'*, i.e., prophet. Although there is some debate as to the origin of this word, scholars generally agree that it derives from an Akkadian root, meaning "to call." The word could be identifying the prophet as one who is called by the Father, the one who calls men in My name, or one who calls to Me on behalf of men. In the Old Testament, each of the above descriptions was characteristic of the prophet, and it might be best to think of the term as implying all three aspects.

The final two terms applied to Old Testament prophets are derived from Hebrew roots for "sight." *Ro'eh* is an active participle of the verb "to see" and is always translated "seer" in Scripture. The second term, *hozeh*, is an active participle of another verb for "seeing" which has no English equivalent. It is sometimes translated "seer" (I Chronicles 29:29) and sometimes "prophet" (Isaiah 30:10). This kind of prophet had prophetic ability to see the future and warn/declare what the future would be (cf. II Chronicles 29:30). First Chronicles 29:29 seems to prove that these three Hebrew terms distinguish three varieties within the prophetic office, for the verse uses each term of different persons who were prophets. That there are similarities in these three kinds of prophets is evidenced in passages such as Amos 7:12ff., where Amaziah addresses Amos as a *hozel*, asking him to prophesy (nabi') in Judah. Amos on that occasion refused, claiming he was not a *nabi'*.

In the New Testament, two Greek verbs identify prophesying. The word *prophaino* means "to reveal" and includes the idea of predicting the future and revealing the message of God.

The other term, *prothemi*, conveys the meaning "to tell forth," to speak to others on My behalf though not necessarily with a predictive message. The noun *prophetes* was used by the Greeks as early as the fourth century B.C. to identify those who could interpret the oracles of the gods. The word literally refers to one who speaks forth, and was loosely applied to anyone who proclaimed a divine message. The word *prophetes* was used in the Old Testament Greek version (the Septuagint or LXX) to translate both *nabi'* and *ro'eh*. It, therefore, came to be understood by the Jews to refer to one anointed of the Holy Spirit who received revelation from and communicated My message.

One of the early Messianic prophecies of the Old Testament was that God would raise up a Prophet like unto Moses (Deuteronomy 18:15). Although the character of this Prophet came to be the standard by which other prophets were evaluated, the Jews clearly understood the prophecy as Messianic. Many Old Testament prophets engaged in prophecy, but only I possessed the credentials and practiced the ministry of the Prophet in perfection. My ministry gave evidence of all three of the following aspects of prophetic preaching:

Spokesman for God—"For-teller" I am a spokesman for God the Father and so fulfilled the office of the prophet. Everything I said was the Word of God. Also, "His name is called the Word of God" (Revelation 19:13). I consciously said and did the will of the Father while here on earth. I told the religious leaders of My day, "The Son can do nothing of himself, but what he sees the Father do: for what things soever he does, these also does the Son likewise" (John 5:19). Later in the same conversation, I said, "I can of mine own self do nothing: as

I hear, I judge: and my judgment is just; because I seek not mine own will, but the will of the Father who hath sent me" (John 5:30).

Prediction—"Foreteller" Normally, when people think of prophecy, their first idea is that of predicting future events. In My role as fore-teller, I made several prophecies. I told My disciples about the coming of the Holy Spirit (John 14:26), which was fulfilled at Pentecost (Acts 2:1-4). Further, I described the ministry of the Holy Spirit in this age (John 16:13,14) and the details of My own death, burial, and resurrection (Matthew 16:21). Additional predictive teachings dealt with My return (John 14:2,3), the existence of the church (Matthew 16:18), and the course of the church age (Matthew 13).

A Preacher to People—"Forth-teller" A prophet speaks truth boldly to people concerning God. Nicodemus, a Pharisee and ruler of the Jews, acknowledged, "Rabbi, we know that thou art a teacher come from God: for no man can do these miracles that thou doest, except God be with him" (John 3:2). When I taught, "the people were astonished at his doctrine; for he taught them as one having authority" (Matthew 7:28,29). I spoke with authority for God the Father. Several of My extended discourses are recorded in Scripture, including the Sermon on the Mount (Matthew 5-7), the mystery parables (Matthew 13), the Olivet discourse (Matthew 24-25), and the Upper Room discourse (John 13-16).

I am certainly consistent with the prophetic tradition of Israel; and, as such, those who heard Me understood Me to be a prophet (cf. Matthew 14). But I was more than just another prophet; I was the unique Prophet. Although there were many similarities between the other prophets and Myself, there were also differences. The most notable of these was My authority in preaching. A prophet of God almost always prefaced his remarks with the expression "Thus saith the Lord"; but, characteristically, I began by saying, "But I say unto you."

I Am the Anointed Priest

A second anointed office in the Old Testament was the priest. Primarily, the priest acted as man's representative before God. The priest offered a sacrifice upon the altar. Because God the Father is by nature both just and forgiving, the priest could always tell the people God would forgive them if they met His conditions. The priest was a channel of forgiveness, whereas the prophet was usually the channel of judgment. Priests were, by far, more popular than prophets.

The office of the priest was an anointed office because the candidate could not practice this office until he was first dipped in water and anointed with oil. This normally occurred at age thirty, and for twenty years the candidate then served as a functioning priest. It is significant that Luke notes this was My age when I was baptized by John and anointed with the Holy Spirit (cf. Luke 3:23).

The fullest development of New Testament teaching on My priesthood is understandably in the book of Hebrews. There it is demonstrated that I am both a priest and a high priest. My priesthood is considered superior because it follows the order of Melchizedek rather than of Aaron. Some commentators have interpreted this claim to mean that Melchizedek was a Christophany, but it is more likely you should view him as a type of Christ! Actually, "Melchizedek" was not a name but a dynastic title, which may also be applied to Me. This explains why the Scriptures appear to call Melchizedek "Jesus." In reality, they are calling Me "Melchizedek."

The office of the priest was unique in nature. First, if one was a priest, the implication is that he had been called of God to that task. Also, as a priest, he could represent another before God. I am a priest, and I serve two major functions—that of offering sacrifices and that of intercession for you.

I am not only a priest but also the High Priest. In addition to My other responsibilities as a priest, the High Priest was particularly involved in the activities of the Day of Atonement (Leviticus 16) and in the use of the Urim and Thummin (Numbers 27:21). I am Israel's mediator on the Day of Atonement, for I took the blood of the slaughtered goat into the Holy of holies, where he offered propitiation for the nation's sins and effected the atonement or covering of their sin for another year. He wore the Urim and Thummin on his breastplate, which contained the names of the twelve tribes and, as such, represented the nation. By using this means, he alone could discern the will of God for the nation. In contrast with the limited national ministry of Israel's High Priest, Jesus "is the propitiation for your sins: and not for ours only, but also for the sins of the whole world" (I John 2:2).

The names "priest" and "high priest" primarily relate to My redemptive work, for they help explain it within the context of the legal system of Moses. Yet, these titles also relate to My person as I fulfilled the ideal qualifications for these offices. I am in both person and ministry your Priest, High Priest, Propitiation, Mediator, and Guide. Many of My secondary names to some extent belong to the function and office of the priest.

I Am the Anointed King

In the Old Testament one of the designations of the coming Messiah was that of Israel's king (cf. Psalm 2:7; Zechariah 9:9). It is interesting to note Nathanael's recognition of Me as "the Son of God ... the King of Israel" (John 1:49). In the Gospel of Mark, the title "King" occurs six times but always as a term of contempt or derision. It is the Gospel of Matthew that really develops this theme. Matthew begins with My legal genealogy, noting Me to be the legal heir to the throne of David. The number fourteen is particularly emphasized in this genealogy (cf. Matthew 1:17). This is significant for two reasons. First, the numerical value of the name "David" is fourteen. Secondly, fourteen is the product of two times seven, seven being the number of perfection or completeness. Most Jews considered David their most nearly perfect king, and Matthew is introducing the "second David." Although several kings are listed in the genealogy, only David is called king.

In the next chapter of Matthew, the magi looking for Me as a babe ask, "Where is he that is born King of the Jews?" (2:2); Herod responds by inquiring of the chief priests and scribes "where Christ should be born" (2:4). Matthew develops this theme further until he records Me acknowledging, "All power is given unto me in heaven and in earth" (28:18). I am the king with ultimate authority.

When the early church practiced the implications of this aspect of who I am, it was not without negative consequences. They called Me their king (Acts 17:7), recognizing Me alone as the supreme Ruler in their lives; but this was offensive to Rome, who viewed Caesar as both god and king. Much of the later persecution of the church was related to Rome's view that recognition of Me as king was seditious. It is, therefore, significant that the theme of the final book written to the persecuted church is My regal status (cf. Revelation 11:15; 19:16).

I am King. My kingship follows from My deity. Because I am God, I am also king. Paul gave praise to King Jesus: "Unto the King eternal, immortal, invisible, the only wise God, be honor and glory forever and ever" (I Timothy 1:17). In heaven "they sing the song of Moses the servant of God, and the song of the Lamb, saying, Great and marvelous are thy works, Lord God Almighty; just and true are thy ways, thou King of saints" (Revelation 15:3). The Romans considered their Caesar to be a god. Christians, on the other hand, recognized Me alone to be their king. Calling Me "king" implied they believed in My deity.

I have a kingdom. Every king has a domain over which he rules, and I am no exception. I acknowledged, "My kingdom is not of this world" (John 18:36), but I never denied I had a kingdom. It was the custom of the Romans to identify the crime of a condemned man by writing it on a shingle and nailing it on the cross upon which he died. I was executed as "the King of the Jews" (John 19:19). When I return to this earth, I will return to establish My kingdom for a thousand years (Revelation 20:1-6).

I have subjects. I am now a ruler to those who submit their wills to Me. Someday, "at the name of Jesus every knee should bow, of things in heaven, and things in earth and things under the earth, and ... every tongue should confess that Jesus is Lord" (Philippians 2:10,11). Today, those who receive Me as Lord and Savior recognize My kingship in their lives. I taught a parable which equated My disciples with servants (Luke 17:10), and that was the attitude of the early church. They were eager to serve Me, their King.

I AM THE CHRIST IN THE NEW TESTAMENT

Many of the New Testament references to Me must be understood in the context of the Old Testament Messiah. This is the probable meaning when Peter confessed I was "the Christ, the Son of the living God" (Matthew 16:16), and when Caiaphas asked Me whether I was the Christ (Matthew 26:63). On the day of Pentecost, Peter concluded his sermon by declaring Me to be "both Lord and Christ" (Acts 2:36), again to be understood in the context of the Old Testament Messiah.

But "Christ" was also the favorite title of Paul, who ministered primarily among Gentiles that lacked the understanding of the Jews concerning the Messiah. In Paul's letters the title "Christ" took on a special significance—a new dimension.

I did not use the title directly of Myself, although I answered "I am" when people asked Me whether I was the Christ (Mark 14:62), and I approved of others calling Me by that title (John 4:25,26; Matthew 16:16,17). On occasion I also mentioned that My disciples belonged to Me (Mark 9:41; Matthew 23:10).

In his epistles, Paul often used the title "Christ" with the name "Jesus," and when he did so, the order of the names was significant. The name "Christ Jesus" referred to the exalted One who emptied Himself (Philippians 2:5-9), emphasizing My preexistence and having reference to My grace. The reverse order of "Jesus Christ," however, referred to My humanity.

One of the great themes in Paul's epistles was that of the union and communion of the believer with Me. In this connection, he uses the expression "in Christ" 172 times and speaks also of My indwelling the believer. Interestingly enough, it is always "Christ," never "Jesus," that he uses to teach indwelling. Paul's use of My title is foundational to your understanding of the Christian life.

Union with Me—Your Position in Heaven

The expression "in Christ" refers to your union with Me, an aspect of the Christian's experience of salvation. Being "in Christ" is a non-experiential state—that is, it occurs at the moment of salvation in the life of every believer, whether he realizes it or not. This is your position or standing in heaven. In Paul's writings "Christ" becomes My positional name after My resurrection.

The nature of the union between Me and the believer is difficult to define and may be best understood if several aspects of this relationship are described. Although in themselves each aspect falls short of what this union is, together they give a more complete portrait of the nature of this union.

This union is a mystical union, for, in a sense, there is a blending of My life into your life so that, although you remain a distinct person, there is a growing oneness in will and purpose. This union transcends the limits even of the marriage union. By this union you also become My friend (cf. John 15:14,15).

Secondly, there is a legal or federal aspect of this union. In this sense, your union with Me becomes the basis of your justification and adoption. It is legal or federal in the sense that I am your lawyer while I represent you before the divine court. Again, although this is one aspect of our union, it also goes much deeper.

Your union is of an organic nature in which not only do you become a member of My body, but I also becomes a part of you. Furthermore the Christian life is the result of a vital union with Me. It is I living in you, not merely influencing you from without. Because the Holy Spirit is the author of this union, it is a spiritual union.

Moreover, this union is both indissoluble and inscrutable. You are so bonded to Me that you have entered into an indissoluble relationship with Me. My omnipresence makes this union possible. Also, because this union involves the nature of God, there is a sense in which you can never fully understand it.

Finally, the union of you and Me must be regarded as both complete and completed. To speak of a believer partially united with Me is as impossible as to speak of a woman who is only partially pregnant. Although you may grow in the realization of this truth, you are never more deeply united with Me by any means than you are at conversion.

Communion with Me—Your Experience on Earth

Not only are you "in Christ," but I am also in you. This is the basis of your communion with Me, which is an experience of your sanctification. The writings of Paul sometimes use the title "Christ" without the article. Paul does this consistently in order to signify the One who by the Holy Spirit and also His own Person indwells the believer and molds the believer's character into a closer conformity to Me (Romans 8:10; Galatians 2:20; 4:19; Ephesians 3:17). The practical application of this truth results in your abiding in Me.

Many writers distinguish two aspects of abiding in Me. First, it means to have no known sin to hinder your communion or fellowship with Me. Secondly, it assumes that you give all burdens and concerns to Me and rely upon Me for the strength, wisdom, faith, and character you need to meet the particular challenges of life. Not only is My position your position (union), but My life is also your life (communion).

CONCLUSION

When the prophets of Israel and Judah spoke of the coming Messiah, their highest thoughts of Me were those of Prophet, Priest, and King. I function today in each of those offices in the life of the believer. But I am also far more. I am no longer merely "the Christ" but also "Christ," the One in whom you dwell and depend upon for the very essence of your spiritual life. I am the One who lives within you, providing all that is necessary for effective Christian living.

For Discussion:

1. What is the literal meaning of the name Christ? Why was it Paul's favorite name for Me?

2. How did I fulfill My office as prophet?

3. As an anointed priest, how do I minister to you today?

4. Describe the kingdom and My rule as King.

5. God's Word teaches that believers are "in Christ" and I abide in believers. What
    affect does this have on your everyday life?

PART TWO

Groupings of My Names

CHAPTER FOUR

MY OLD TESTAMENT PROPHETIC NAMES

"Philip findeth Nathanael, and saith unto him, We have found Him, of whom Moses in the law, and the prophets, did write, Jesus of Nazareth, the son of Joseph" (John 1:45).

"And beginning at Moses and all the prophets, I expounded unto them, in all the scriptures the things concerning Me" (Luke 24:27).

It often has been said that the Old Testament is where I am concealed and the New Testament is where I am revealed. The Old Testament was the Bible by which the early church preached My gospel to a lost world. Hidden in the pages of law, history, poetry, and prophecy is a wealth of My revelation concerning the names Lord Jesus Christ. I am revealed in every book through types, metaphors, analogies, and indisputable titles. Although it would be impossible to consider every title in a single chapter, in this chapter several of My principal titles in the Old Testament are discussed. Some important Old Testament names are omitted here because they are covered in later chapters.

SHILOH

Shiloh is one of My earliest names in Genesis that applies to the coming Messiah. As Jacob was blessing his sons and prophesying concerning the twelve tribes of Israel, he said: "The sceptre shall not depart from Judah, nor a lawgiver from between his feet, until I, Shiloh, come; and unto Me shall the gathering of the people be" (Genesis 49:10).

My name *Shiloh* means "peace maker" and closely relates to one of Isaiah's birth names for Me, "the Prince of Peace" (Isaiah 9:6). This prophecy affirms that I, Shiloh, would come from the royal tribe of Judah, wield a temporal scepter, and possess a sovereignty of a different character.

PROPHET

The great prophet in the history of Israel was Moses, although before he died, he prophesied of My future that the Jews came to understand to be Me, the coming Messiah. "The Lord thy God will raise up unto you a Prophet from the midst of thee, of thy brethren, like unto me; unto him ye shall hearken" (Deuteronomy 18:15). I am the prophet who would speak as a forthteller, preaching a message; as a for-teller, preaching for the Father; and as a fore-teller, predicting things to come. My preaching conformed to each aspect of this prophetic preaching.

THE BRANCH

Your English Bible translates three Hebrew words "branch" as My name or title. The first word, *tsemach*, literally refers to a green shoot or sprout growing out of an old stump. A similar word, *netser*, was used of a small, fresh green twig. A third word, translated "rod" in Isaiah 11:1, was *choter*, this refers to a shoot growing out of a cut-down stump. These three words describe Me as "the Branch."

My title had both positive and negative connotations. A puzzling verse in Matthew refers to an Old Testament prophecy to the effect, "I shall be called a Nazarene" (Matthew 2:23). To be called a Nazarene by those living outside Nazareth was insulting, for the town had a reputation as the city of garbage. Even one of My first disciples asked, "Can any good thing come out of Nazareth?" (John 1:46). But the puzzling thing about this verse is that no verse in the Old Testament identifies Nazareth as My home. Most commentators suggest Matthew was here alluding to one of the Branch prophecies, having noted the similarity of sound between *netser* and Nazareth.

Isaiah did use the word *netzer* in a negative sense when he said of the king of Babylon, "But thou art cast out of thy grave like an abominable branch" (Isaiah 14:19). Here the word describes a useless shoot cut off a tree and left to rot. Although Isaiah's use of the word in this context does not specifically refer to Me, it does demonstrate how Matthew could have understood a Branch prophecy to imply that I would have to live with the reputation of being a Nazarene.

Positively, these words for "Branch" are used in four ways corresponding to the four Gospels in the New Testament. First, I am Christ the King—Branch. This corresponds to the Gospel of Matthew, which emphasizes My life as the King of the Jews. Jeremiah noted, "Behold, the days come, saith the Lord, that I will raise unto David a righteous Branch, and a King shall reign and prosper, and shall execute judgment and justice in the earth" (Jeremiah 23:5). This title specifically applies to My coming kingdom during My millennial reign.

I am also spoken of as a Servant Branch. This corresponds to the Gospel of Mark, which portrays Me as the Servant of the Lord. The prophet Zechariah announced, "Behold, I will bring forth my servant, the BRANCH" (Zechariah 3:8). I was not only a king but a servant. Several passages in Isaiah more fully describe Me as the Servant of the Father.

The next Branch described Me as a man. This corresponds to the unique emphasis of the Gospel of Luke, which eighty times refers to Me as the Son of man. Again, it was the prophet Zechariah who announced this aspect of the Branch. "Behold the man whose name is The BRANCH; and he shall grow up out of his place, and he shall build the temple of the Lord" (Zechariah 6:12).

The last aspect of Me, the Branch, is that I, the Lord Myself, am the Branch. This corresponds to the emphasis of the Gospel of John, which begins with a statement as to My deity as the Word. "In that day shall the branch of the Lord be beautiful and glorious" (Isaiah 4:2). Again, this name specifically applies to My deity.

THE DESIRE OF ALL NATIONS

Perhaps no preacher in history left behind such a brief record of ministry with as great accomplishment as the prophet Haggai. The book which records his name has five sermons that range in length from a single line to several verses. Yet, it was primarily the preaching of this prophet that led to the resumption of work and completion of the second temple in Jerusalem. Because some Jews had seen the previous temple in all its physical splendor, they became discouraged as they saw the builders erecting a smaller wood frame structure. Haggai knew the people were failing to realize it was not the architecture of a building but rather My presence that made a building a holy place. To encourage the people, Haggai prophesied of the days when "the desire of all nations shall come" (Haggai 2:7).

Commentators discuss the meaning of this phrase "desire of all nations." Some argue Haggai meant the wealth of other nations—that is, the desirable things of those nations—would someday be brought to this second temple. A more probable interpretation is that it means My title Christ. I will come to the temple that seemed so insignificant in the eyes of some of the workers.

Jewish writers have noted that the second temple lacked five objects which were present in the first temple: the ark of the covenant with its mercy seat or place of propitiation, the tables of the law, the holy fire, the sacred oracle in the breastplate of the high priest, and the Shekinah glory of God. Although I did not give these things to the remnant that returned and then built the second temple, I did promise to come as the "desire of all nations"; I was all these things and more.

I am the reality of which the ark was only the type. I am only the place of propitiation, i.e., "the propitiation for your sins" (I John 2:2). The early Christians applied the title "Lawgiver" to Me (James 4:12). I am the "Urim and Thummin," and your "High Priest." But above all these things, I am the incarnate "Shekinah glory of God." As the Apostle John noted, "And I, the Word, was made flesh, and dwelt among you (and you beheld My glory, the glory as of the only begotten of the Father), full of grace and truth" (John 1:14). The Shekinah glory was indeed absent at the dedication of the second temple, but eventually it came in My presence as Christ. The "desire of all nations" came; I am the fullness of the Godhead, and I dwelt or tabernacled among you.

Although this prophecy had partial fulfillment in My first advent, many commentators point out that the context of this prophecy applies to My second coming. In the millennium I will be King and Lord of the nations. In that sense, I am the "desire of all nations" yet to come. However, in a sense I am the "desirable one of all nations" today, since Christians around the world echo the final prayer of the Scriptures, "Even so, come, Lord Jesus" (Revelation 22:20).

THE ENSIGN OF THE PEOPLES

One of My many titles in the book of Isaiah is "an ensign of the peoples" (Isaiah 11:10). Of the seven times the word "ensign" appears in Scripture, six are singular and found in the prophecy of Isaiah. The word itself refers to a national flag to which people rally. The flag is a symbol of the nation, and loyalty to that flag is the most common form of patriotism.

While Elmer Towns served as President of Winnipeg Bible College, the Canadian government redesigned a new national flag. At the time a great debate arose over the proposed action. Many Canadians remembered fighting for liberty in World War II and the Korean War under the old Red Ensign. To change that flag seemed unpatriotic and an attack on the national heritage of Canadians. Today, almost five decades later, most Canadians feel a sense of deep-seated patriotism when they see their new Maple Leaf flag blowing in the wind. Just as the old Red Ensign was an untouchable symbol of the nation in the early sixties, so many Canadians would respond the same way if the government tried to change the flag today and abandon the Maple Leaf flag.

As a nation rallies around its flag, Christians rally around Me. I am their flag, their symbol of loyalty. The history of the church is a record of various conflicts and debates over different interpretations of doctrine. But true Christianity has always been grounded in their agreement concerning Me. There were times when good men thought it wrong to baptize, wrong to send out missionaries, or wrong to be involved in political action, but they have always found a rallying point around Me and the work I accomplished. I have been the Ensign to which they have been drawn.

As "an ensign for the peoples," I am not just the flag which brings a group of Christians from one country together but, rather, the flag which brings believers from all places together. Commenting on this title of Christ, Charles J. Rolls exclaimed,

- What a distinction! To be high above all principality and power.
- What a recognition! To be revered by myriad hosts of men and angels.
- What a coronation! To be crowned Lord of lords and King of kings.
- What a commemoration! To be admired in all them that believe.

45

EL SHADDAI — THE ALMIGHTY

When I appeared to Abraham to confirm My covenant with him, I revealed Myself to the ninety-nine-year old man of faith as *El Shaddai* (Genesis 17:1). Linguists do not agree about the etymology of this title and usually suggest one of three possibilities. Some link the word to the Hebrew *shadad*, meaning "to devastate," and argue the title lays emphasis on My irresistible power. Others believe the word relates the Akkadian word *shadu*, meaning "mountain," and argue the title means something like "I am God of the Mountains." The third and most probable meaning of this word is based on its relationship to the Hebrew word *shad*, meaning "breast."

El Shaddai is naturally My tender title. Scripture uses it exclusively of Me in relation to My children. When trying to explain more fully the implications of this name, some writers have spoken of "My mother-love." To the child held to his mother's breast, the mother is the all-sufficient one who provides both the physical necessities and emotional support the child needs. Similarly I, El Shaddai, am the all-sufficient One in the believer's experience. I have been accurately described as "the God who is enough."

El Shaddai was Job's favorite name for Me. Thirty-one of its forty-eight occurrences in Scripture appear in the book of Job. For Job in the midst of his suffering and despair, I as El Shaddai was enough. This title suggests supplying the need and comforting the hurt. Over the years, many Christians have discovered My true nature of *El Shaddai* only in their darkest hours. When you understand My name, you can grow in your Christian experience, knowing My tenderness so you can confess with Job, "Though he slay me, yet will I trust in him" (Job 13:15).

CONCLUSION

Throughout the Old Testament the prophets of God looked forward to the day when I their coming Messiah would arrive. As I continued to reveal more and more about Myself, different names describe Me more accurately. Hundreds of such names appear in the pages of the Old Testament but they describe only part of My character and nature. Although My names were given to nourish a sense of anticipation and expectation, you can enjoy them even more for now. I am proven to be far more than what the prophets could have imagined.

For Discussion:

1. What is probably My earliest name in the Old Testament? What do you know about your Savior from this title?
2. One of My favorite titles in the prophets was Branch. How am I your Branch?
3. Haggai called Me "the desire of all nations." How do I fulfill this title?
4. Isaiah called Me "the ensign of the people." What should be your reaction to this name?
5. Share an experience when you realized that I was your El Shaddai.

CHAPTER FIVE

MY SALVATIONAL NAMES

"For I know that my redeemer liveth, and that he shall stand at the latter day upon the earth" (Job 19:25).

"Let the words of my mouth, and the meditation of my heart, be acceptable in thy sight, O LORD, my strength, and my redeemer" (Psalm 19:14).

Theologians refer to certain of My names and titles as the soteriological titles because they have particular reference to My work in salvation. These names describe My "salvational duties" because they are the names which reveal or clarify your salvation more fully. Although the Bible speaks of salvation in three tenses (past, present and future), the names in this chapter refer primarily to salvation past—that is, to your conversion rather than your sanctification and eventual My glorification. You might designate these names as evangelistic names, for they tend to explain the evangel or gospel of salvation.

REDEEMER

When you think of the doctrine of salvation, sooner or later you must consider the concept of redemption. It is a little surprising, however, that My title "Redeemer" is never used of Me in the New Testament although its verbal form occurs both in the Gospels and Epistles in connection with My work of redemption (Luke 1:68; 24:21; Galatians 3:13; 4:5; Titus 2:14; I Peter 1:18; Revelation 5:9; 14:3,4). This name for Me was, nevertheless, a popular title in the Old Testament, particularly in the Psalms (Job 19:25; Psalm 19:14).

Although the New Testament does not call Me "Redeemer," it certainly emphasizes My work of redemption throughout. The term "redemption" comes from a word which means "to buy back." I gave My blood as a ransom for sin; by it I redeemed the lost (I Peter 1:18-20). In the context of soteriology, the price of redemption is blood which is paid to procure the remission of your sins (Hebrews 9:12,22). The Greek words for "redeemed" denote the purchase of servants in the ancient slave market. The Bible however applies the terms to the redemption of all men.

First, the Bible teaches that I purchased the sinner in the marketplace. The verb *agorazo* means "to go to the marketplace (*agora*) and pay the price for a slave." The verb was common in deeds of sale and generally meant the paying of a price for a group of slaves. Those who were "sold under sin" are redeemed (Galatians 3:10). Each of the following Scriptures uses the term *agorazo*: Revelation 14:3,4 speaks of the 144,000 as those redeemed from the earth; Revelation 5:9 notes that My blood was the price paid for redemption; and II Peter 2:1 shows that I redeemed (paid the price) not only for the saved but also for the false teachers. *Agorazo* is simply the payment, the purchase price—the price of redemption, which is blood.

A second word in the Bible for "redemption" is *ekagorazo*, meaning "to buy out from the marketplace." The prefix *ek* means "out." Therefore, this term refers to the fact that I paid the price with My blood and bought the slave "out of the marketplace" of sin. The slave was never again exposed to sale (Galatians 3:13). When I took mankind out from under the Law, I placed them in a different relationship to the Father by providing for him the opportunity to become an adopted son of the Father (Galatians 4:5). *Ekagorazo* emphasizes the removal of the curse of the Law (Galatians 3:13; 4:5).

The third word which refers to redemption is *lutrao*. This word means "to pay the price for the slave and then release him" (Galatians 4:5). It emphasizes the freedom that I bring to those whom I redeemed. This verb suggests that I work to separate you completely from all sin (Titus 2:14).

A consideration of each of these terms and the contexts in which they appear in the New Testament indicates I have provided redemption for all people by the shedding of My own blood (Hebrews 9:12).

That redemption includes the price of redemption (*agorazo*), removal from the marketplace of sin (*ekagorazo*), and the provision of liberty to the redeemed (*lutrao*). This is My work as the Redeemer. But the sinner is not prepared to go to heaven until he responds by faith to the Redeemer.

SAVIOR

It is interesting that Scripture rarely uses the name "Savior" for Me, especially in view of the fact that "Savior" is fundamental to all I am and did. At My birth the angel announced, "For unto you is born this day in the city of David a Savior, which is Christ the Lord" (Luke 2:11). Early in My ministry, a group of Samaritans concluded the same truth and told the woman who met Me at Sychar's well, "Now we believe, not because of thy saying: for we have heard you ourselves, and know that you are indeed the Christ, the Savior of the world" (John 4:42). But these are the only two instances in the Gospels of this title being applied to Me. I was seldom called "Savior" in the Epistles although both Peter (Acts 5:3 1) and Paul (Acts 13:23) used this title for Me in their preaching.

Men have wondered why this name that embodies the very essence of My work should be almost neglected by the apostles. Two reasons suggest themselves. First, the apostles may have been trying to avoid a major confrontation with Roman authorities. One of the titles of Caesar was "Savior of the World." A second reason for its infrequent use may have been that was all I am and do in My saving work led the New Testament writers to take the title for granted. Both Peter and Paul used this title in an evangelistic appeal where they were trying to explain the fundamentals of the gospel. If this were characteristic of the evangelical preaching of the early church, we would not expect a special emphasis in the epistles, which were written largely to correct problems in the church. The emphasis on Me as Savior may be absent because early believers widely understood and accepted it.

The Greek word *soter* means "a Savior," "deliverer" or "preserver." It is My title as well as used to describe the Father. It shares a common root with the verb *sozo*, which is the most commonly used expression of conversion in the Scriptures. This verb is used in three tenses in the New Testament to describe complete and full salvation. First, the believer has been saved from the guilt and penalty of sin. Secondly, you are being saved from the habit and dominion of sin.

Thirdly, you will be saved at My return from all the bodily infirmities and curse that result from sin.

THE LAMB OF GOD

In the first twenty-six books of the New Testament only John the Baptist uses the title "Lamb of God." The expression occurs twenty-six times in the final book of the New Testament. When we think of the book of Revelation, we usually think of Me as "the Lion of the Tribe of Judah"—that is, the coming king, but the most frequent title of Mine in that book is "the Lamb." The reason is that My coming as king is possible only because of My sacrifice as a lamb.

Being the son of a priest, John the Baptist was no doubt familiar with the importance of the lamb offered every morning and evening in a whole burnt offering. He was acquainted as well with the other sacrifices, including Passover. This title was probably derived from Isaiah's description of the "Suffering Servant of the Lord" (Isaiah 53) and the levitical system of sacrifice in Israel. Just as a lamb was offered on the altar for sin, so the Lamb of God would be offered for the sin of the world.

John predicted that the Lamb of God would take away sin. The verb *airon*, translated "taketh away," conveys the idea of taking something up and carrying it away and, in that sense, destroying it. I took away sin by bearing it in My own body (I Peter 2:24), and so, I removed your transgressions as far as the east is from the west (Psalm 103:12). Even before the cross John spoke of Me as the Lamb already taking away sin.

At least ten times Scripture speaks about the taking away of sin:

WHEN I, THE LAMB OF GOD, TAKE AWAY SIN

1. Before the foundation of the world (Revelation 13:8)
2. At the Fall of man (Genesis 3:15)
3. With My offering of a sacrifice (Genesis 4:7)
4. On the Day of Atonement (Leviticus 16:34)
5. At a time of national repentance (II Chronicles 7:14)
6. During My public ministry (John 1:29)
7. On the cross (I Peter 2:24)

8. At conversion (Romans 6:6)
9. At My Second Coming (Romans 8:18-23)
10. At the end of the millennium (Revelation 20:15; 21:8)

PROPITIATION

Another one of My titles which relates to the Lamb of God is "The Propitiation." The Greek word *hilaskornai* occurred in pagan literature to describe the sacrifices offered to idols in order to appease their wrath. The translators of the Septuagint used this word in a technical sense to identify the mercy seat, the place of reconciliation between Me and men. The term conveys the idea of a full satisfaction to appease the wrath of the Father. I bore the full brunt of the Father's wrath, and so I am the Propitiation for sin (I John 2:2).

In an effort to escape the connotation that the wrath of the Father must be appeased, some translators prefer to translate this term "expiation." But this view fails to recognize the offensiveness of sin in the eyes of the Father and the reality of His wrath against sin.

That I am your Propitiation has deep meaning for every believer. First it is the basis of your salvation. The "sinner's prayer," "God be merciful to me a sinner" (Luke 18:13), is literally, "God be propitious to me the sinner." Also, it is the incentive for your love for other Christians. "Herein is love, not that you loved Me, but that I loved you, and the Father sent Me as the propitiation for your sins. Beloved, I so loved you, you ought also to love one another" (I John 4:10,11).

THE LAST ADAM

The Apostle Paul taught that the human race consisted of two groups—those who were "in Adam" and those who were "in Me." In presenting this contrast, he used several of My comparative names, including "the Last Adam" (I Corinthians 15:45) and "the Second Man" (I Corinthians 15:47). These two related titles are fundamental to the doctrine of imputation, the means by which the Father applies your sin to Me and My righteousness to you.

When you speak of "the headship of the race," you do so in two senses. First, Adam was the Federal Head of the race and when he sinned, you sinned in the sense that when your representative government takes a course of action, you also take that action. Secondly,

53

Adam was the Seminal Head of the race in that he was the physical father of the human race. When Adam sinned, he became a sinner by nature. You as Adam's descendants also sin, much as the child of a mother who is a drug addict may take a drug when the mother takes a drug.

I, the Last Adam and Second Man, am the head of a new race in the same way Adam was the head of the old race. When I died for you, I paid the price for your sin. When I rose from the dead, I did so as a quickening or life-giving spirit, able and willing to impart new life to all who come to Me.

History and society are the result of two men and their respective acts. Adam, by disobedience, plunged this world into the slavery of sin. I, Jesus, by obedience, brought this world back to the Father. Because of what the first Adam did, you need to be saved. Because of what I, the Last Adam did, you may be saved.

AUTHOR OF ETERNAL SALVATION

When describing Me, the writer to the Hebrews notes, "I became the author of eternal salvation unto all them that obey Me" (Hebrews 5:9). The Greek word used here for salvation is *aitios*, which denotes that which causes something else. I am the "Author of Salvation" as one might be an author of a novel. The author knows all that is to be written before the book is published. He develops the plan of the book, its underlying thesis, the characters, and plot or story line. And when the book is complete, it contains a part of the author who invested part of his life in the book.

When you speak of Me as "the Author of Eternal Salvation," this illustration is accurate only in part. I am not merely the formal cause of salvation, I am the efficacious and active cause of it. Not only is salvation caused or effected by Me, but I am Salvation itself (Luke 2:30; 3:6). Although an author may invest a part of himself in his book, you cannot say the book is the author. But I am that of which I am the author. When the Scriptures reveal Me as the "Author of Eternal Salvation," it emphasizes not only My ability to save but also My power to keep.

Closely related to this title are several titles which make use of the Greek word *archegos*, translated in Scripture as "prince," "author," and "captain." This is the key word in the titles "Prince of life" (Acts 3:15), "a Prince and a Savior" (Acts 5:31), "the captain of their salvation" (Hebrews 2:10), and "the author and finisher of our faith" (Hebrews 12:2). The term signifies one who takes the lead in something or provides the first occasion of anything. In his English translation of the Scriptures, Moffat consistently translates this word "pioneer." Although translated "author" once in the New Testament, the word really stresses quality of leadership; it does not necessarily mean that the cause originated with the leader. The emphasis here is that of My primacy. As the *aitios*, I originate and provide eternal salvation for all who will come to Me. As the *archegos*, I lead you into eternal salvation. In this way I am the Captain of Salvation, the Prince of Life, and the Pioneer (Author) of your Faith.

MEDIATOR

I am also called the "mediator" by the Apostle Paul (I Timothy 2:5; cf. also Hebrews 8:6; 9:15; 12:24). In the first century this was both a legal and commercial term. It differs from My title as your "Advocate" in that the "Mediator" is impartial; I represent both parties equally. Only I could be the mediator between God and man because only I am both God and man. The Greek word *mesites* literally means "a go-between" and is used in two ways in the New Testament. First, I am the Mediator in that I mediate between God and man to effect a reconciliation (I Timothy 2:5). Secondly, I am the mediator of a better covenant (Hebrews 8:6), the new testament (Hebrews 9:15), and the new covenant (Hebrews 12:24) in the sense that I act as a guarantor so I secure that which would otherwise be unobtainable.

CONCLUSION

No wonder the hymn writer exclaimed, "I will sing of my Redeemer"! The more you understand what the Bible describes as "so great salvation," the more you appreciate My salvational names. Some speak of My work in saving them. I am "the Redeemer," "Savior," and "Mediator." Others speak of My Person in saving you. I am "the Lamb of God" and "the Propitiation for Your Sins." Still others reveal Me who both produces and is your salvation. I am "the Last Adam," "the Second Man," and "the Author of Eternal Salvation." All of your questions concerning your salvation are answered in My names.

But, the meaning of My salvational names must be applied to your life. I am the propitiation for the sins of the whole world, but you may call Me "your Propitiation" only when you have received Me by faith to pay for your sin. I am your "Mediator" in the deepest sense when you believe on Me as Savior. Knowing My salvational names carry with it a grave responsibility—that of being certain you have obtained so great a salvation. And if you have, knowing My salvational names provides for you a tremendous privilege, for you can introduce others to Me who loves them and gave Myself for them.

For Discussion:

1. From what have I redeemed you? What was the payment or ransom?
2. Why was the name Savior neglected by the apostles? How can you avoid taking My title and work for granted?
3. How should you feel and act in response to My work as the Lamb of God?
4. When I am called Propitiation, what have I accomplished? What influence should this have on your life?
5. Why am I called the last Adam? Are you under the headship of the first or last Adam?
6. Give as many of My titles as possible that relate to your salvation. Discuss briefly
   what each title suggests about salvation.

CHAPTER SIX

MY BIRTH NAMES

"Therefore the Father Himself shall give you a sign: Behold, a virgin shall conceive, and bear a son, and you shall call My name Immanuel" (Isaiah 7.14).

"For unto you a child is born, unto you a son is given: and the government shall be upon My shoulder: and My name shall be called Wonderful, Counselor, The Mighty God, The Everlasting Father, The Prince of Peace" (Isaiah 9:6).

My virgin conception was prophesied long before My birth in Bethlehem and, when understood correctly, is one of the foundational doctrines of Christian faith. Genesis 3:15 is the first reference to My coming; embryonically it anticipated the virgin birth by calling Me "the seed of the woman." My miraculous birth was not so much in the birth but, rather, in My supernatural conception. There are five persons in Scripture with supernatural origins. Adam was created with neither male nor female parents. Eve's origin involved a man but no female. Isaac was born to parents both of whom were beyond the age in which they could physically produce children. John the Baptist was born to parents who were well into old age. But the greatest of the supernatural origins was Mine, whose birth involved a virgin but no man.

As miraculous as My virgin birth was, the real significance of the event is that it marked My incarnation. In the words of John, "the Word was made flesh" (John 1:14). Even Isaiah, the prophet of the virgin birth, alluded to the incarnation when he differentiated between a human child born and the divine Son given (Isaiah 9:6). My birth, celebrated each year at Christmas, marks the time when I emptied Myself to become man. Though I always remained God, while on earth, My glory was veiled, and I chose voluntarily to limit Myself in the independent use of My non-moral attributes.

One of the tasks of the parents of a newborn baby is to give that child a name. Usually the parents will spend several months discussing possible names they may or may not choose. Often friends and relatives will suggest names they think are suitable. The concern of many parents is to choose a name that expresses their aspirations for their child or suggests by association a positive role model for the child. When a name is chosen, it has a special significance to the proud parents of the newborn baby.

Several of My names and titles were given Me in the context of My birth. It is almost as though the prophets sought for the ideal name for Me as they anticipated My coming to this world. In this chapter, you will look at several of what may be called "My Birth Names."

THE DAYSPRING FROM ON HIGH

When Zacharias prophesied at the birth of his son John, he called his son "the prophet of the Highest" (Luke 1:76). But the emphasis of his prophecy focused upon Me, the One he called "the dayspring from on high" (Luke 1:78). It was to be characteristic of the life and ministry of John that he, "a bright and shining light," should seem dim in comparison to Me, who was the "Light of the World."

The word "Dayspring" is a translation of the Greek word *anatole*, literally meaning "a rising of light" or "sunrise." The place of the dayspring was the point along the eastern horizon at which the sun rose, a place which changed with the passing seasons (cf. Job 38:12). By implication, the term came to mean the east—that is, the direction of the sunrise (cf. Matthew 2:1). Zacharias used it metaphorically of Me, the One through whom the true Light shone, not only to Israel but to all the world.

There is something unique about this particular sunrise. This dayspring originated "from on high" (*ex hupsos*). *Hupsos* refers not only to height but to the idea of being raised to a high or exalted state (cf. James 1:9). It closely relates to the adjective *hupsistos*, the word which describes John as the prophet "of the Highest" (Luke 1:76). The use of this particular term in this context implies that this was uniquely a divinely appointed or exalted sunrise. Perhaps the sun shone just a little brighter on the morning following My birth as the Dayspring from on High.

The appearance of Me as the Dayspring from on High on the horizon of human history produced significant effects. Its shining exposes your sin. Its warmth revitalizes your hope in sorrow. And its light redirects your steps.

The Revelation of Your Sin

In speaking of the visitation of the Dayspring from on High, Zacharias suggested My purpose, "To give light to those who sit in darkness" (Luke 1:79). One of the effects of a natural sunrise is the illumination of an otherwise dark world. Someone has observed that the darkest hour of night comes just before the dawn. There is certainly a spiritual reality in the application of this truth. The Greek word *skotia* is used in the New Testament not only of physical darkness but also of the spiritual darkness of sin. Of the various Greek words that describe darkness, this word indicates the darkest. So, the effect of sin in the life results in not a mere gloominess but a blinding darkness in which any measure of illuminating light is absent. So dark is the darkness of sin that even sin itself is hidden by the darkness.

The cresting of the sun over the mountains along the eastern horizon first makes visible the shadows in the night and then that which the shadows hid in the night. My appearance as the Dayspring from on High produces first the light of conviction in a soul darkened by sin and then floods the soul with gospel light, so that you can understand spiritual truth (II Corinthians 4:4-6). When I was challenged to pass sentence upon the woman caught in the act of adultery, I merely spoke the word that brought conviction to the conscience of each accuser (John 8:9). In that place John uses the verb *eleochomenoi*, translated "convicted," but literally means "to bring to light and expose." Just as one might hold a letter up to the light to expose its contents, so I exposed the sin of self-righteous people by My penetrating light.

Your Revitalization in Sorrow

There is yet another effect of the natural sunrise which finds a spiritual counterpart in My Dayspring from on High. The light and warmth of the early morning sun is that which revitalizes life on earth.

As the light of the sun rises on the eastern horizon, the flowers of the field once again turn and open to absorb the benefits it offers. The animals which hid from the darkness and dangers of the night begin to come out of the caves and hollow logs to enjoy the day. The people of primitive lands begin to remove the coverings which kept them warm in the night as the sunlight of a new day announces yet another opportunity to work while it is still light. It is, therefore, not without significance that Zacharias noted the shining of light to those who walked in "the shadow of death" (Luke 1:79).

Light was one of My great symbols in Messianic prophecy. According to Isaiah, the Messianic light was to shine brightest in Galilee of the Gentiles, upon people who walked in darkness (Isaiah 9:1,2). Often those who find themselves hiding in the shadows are the ones who benefit most from the light. Darkness aids the criminal in the successful accomplishment of his crime. For that reason people all over the world fear the night and eagerly await morning. The pilgrims of Israel understood the significance of the coming morning and My greater significance as their coming Lord. As they sang their hymns of worship, they testified, "My soul waits for the Lord more than they that watch for the morning: I say, more than they that watch for the morning" (Psalm 130:6).

In your sorrow and hurt, I, the Dayspring from on High, shine to revitalize light and warmth. How often has the discouraged Christian, groping in the shadows of even death itself, found in My heavenly sunrise the source of strength he needs to continue? How encouraging the thought that in your constant struggle with the darkness of this world, I, the Dayspring from on High, shine a light which the darkness cannot hide. French theologian Frederic Godet used to think of the Dayspring in the context of an eastern caravan which had lost its way in the night but, while sitting down and expecting death, soon noticed a star begin to rise over the horizon, providing the light which would lead them to the place of safety. Unquestionably, there are and will be many times in life when, like those discouraged traders, the believer would resign to defeat but for My appearance as morning light from heaven.

The Redirection of Your Steps

A third benefit of My appearance of the Dayspring from on High is the redirection of your steps, "to guide your feet into the way of peace" (Luke 1:79). The implication is that My light of sunrise enables you to see how to walk a straight path that leads to "the way of peace." "A man's heart devises his way: but I, the Lord, directs his steps" (Proverbs 16:9). That your steps often need redirection is self-evident to any and all who have attempted to live the Christian life. The Word of God is My instrument to give direction in your life (Psalm 119:105). As you continue to walk by faith in the Christian life, you come to know experientially "My peace, which passes all understanding" (Philippians 4:7).

The Redemption of Your Souls

The priority in the life of John the Baptist was "to give knowledge of salvation unto My people for the remission of their sins" (Luke 1:77). But that was possible only because of My visitation as the Dayspring "through My tender mercy as your God" (Luke 1:78). "My tender mercy" is literally "the mercy of My heart," meaning that mercy which springs from the innermost seat of My self-existence. In My mercy, the benefits of your redemption are found. Zacharias was concerned both with the national deliverance of Israel (Luke 1:68-75) and the personal salvation of those who come to Me by faith (Luke 1:76-79). Both of these aspects of salvation will materialize by My visitation from the Dayspring.

The Scriptures view a visitation by God either positively or negatively. When I visit a people in My wrath, it is a time of great and severe judgment. When I visit a people in My mercy, it is a time of salvation. The psalmist said your prayer must be, "O visit me with salvation" (Psalm 106:4).

How penetrating is the light of My brilliant heavenly sunrise! It reaches into the darkest areas of your life, revealing your sin. When convicted of sin by that light, you begin to understand its horror and the inevitable penalty—death itself. But that is also the light which revitalizes you in your sorrow. If you were to respond to that light while you remain in your darkness, you would no doubt stumble and fall or miss the narrow way altogether. So it is My same sunrise which provides light to redirect your steps. The ultimate effect of My light is the redemption of your souls. Understanding and experiencing these few benefits of My Dayspring from on High will cause your hearts to praise and worship Me who granted to you this merciful visitation.

IMMANUEL (EMMANUEL)

When I gave the faithless Ahaz an opportunity to ask Me for a sign to encourage his faith, he was so apathetic to My things; he refused to accept My gracious offer. My purpose was not to defeat Ahaz, but give him a sign. He chose not to ask for a sign which I had offered him. "Behold, a virgin shall conceive, and bear a son, and shall call his name Immanuel" (Isaiah 7:14). That unusual name for Me captured the highest of ideals in the religious life of the pious Jew. It was an affirmation of the highest of blessings, "I am with you."

Whenever I called a person or group to a seemingly impossible challenge, I reminded them of My all-sufficient promise, "Certainly I will be with thee." Moses was to deliver Israel from Egypt, but I was with him (Exodus 3:12). Joshua was to conquer the Promised Land, but I was with him (Joshua 1:5). Throughout Israel's history, every effective judge and king owed his success to the fact that "I, the Lord, was with him." When Nebuchadnezzar looked into the fire, expecting to see the flames consuming the physical remains of three faithful Hebrews, he saw them surviving the flames, and I, the Lord, was with them. When the remnant returned to rebuild the temple, they were motivated to action by the prophet's reminder, "I am with you, saith the Lord" (Haggai 1:13).

In contrast to the Old Testament promise of My presence, the absence or withdrawal of My presence, when noted, is a foreboding warning of disasters to come. Cain went out from My presence to found a society so degenerate I had to destroy it with a flood. Samson woke in the lap of Delilah, not knowing that I, the Spirit, had departed, and he was captured by the Philistines. Because of his constant disobedience to My revealed will, Saul lost his unique relationship with the Holy Spirit, and I replaced the Holy Spirit with an evil spirit.

But in the New Testament, that relationship between Me and you changed and intensified. The Christian has an unprecedented relationship with Me. In this regard, the name Immanuel (Emmanuel) signifies something special in the Christian's life.

First, it, is an incarnational name. "I, the Word, was made flesh, and dwelt among you" (John 1:14); in a unique way in human history, "I was God with You." Secondly, it is a dispensational name. The unique "in Christ" and "Christ in you" relationship in this present dispensation of grace is My promise to you.

The Effect of My Name, Immanuel

In every art and industry of mankind, Christians have found a place where their relationship with Me can be both enjoyed and expressed. My presence is effective, first, in producing a deeper communion with Me. The Christian life may be summarized in two areas of experience—the point of salvation and the process of sanctification. Before salvation, I was present knocking at the door (Revelation 3:20) and waiting to be received (John 1:12). In sanctification, I am present dwelling within (John 14:23) and continuously completing My work I began at conversion (Philippians 1:6).

The "God with Us" relationship is effective also in securing My definite conquest for you. The Christian is engaged in a spiritual warfare which cannot be waged, much less won, without Me, Immanuel, My presence with you. As Joshua prepared to conquer the Promised Land, a type of Christian experience, he was first assured of My presence (Joshua 1:5). Joseph was tempted unsuccessfully by Potiphar's wife, the Scripture is both prefaced and concluded with the remark, "The Lord was with Joseph" (Genesis 39:2,21). You are victorious in Me because I am working in you (Philippians 2:13), and you are in Me (Romans 8:37).

Thirdly, My deep consolation flows from Me with assurance to perplexity (Genesis 28:15), encouraging My servants (Exodus 3:12), a fortification for the timid (Jeremiah 1:8), a confidence for the teacher (Matthew 28:20), a rest for the pilgrim (Exodus 33:14), and a strength for the fearful (Hebrews 13:5,6).

The Experience of My Name, Immanuel

There is an important distinction between the believer's union with Me (which exists as a result of the baptism of the Holy Spirit and My work on the cross, both applied at salvation) and the believer's communion with Me, by which he experiences and enjoys the results of our union. You enjoy the benefits of the name Immanuel—God with You—as you respond in obedience to My multifaceted call in your life.

The first aspect of the call is the call to salvation. Throughout the New Testament, this call has a universal appeal; for I "will have all men to be saved, and to come unto the knowledge of the truth" (I Timothy 2:4) and, therefore, I "now command all men everywhere to repent" (Acts 17:30, cf. also II Peter 3:9).

Secondly, there is a call to sanctification. By sanctification I set you apart to holiness. It involves all three aspects of biblical separation (cf. I Thessalonians 1:9). First, you are separated to Me. Further, you are separated from sin. Finally, you are separated to service. I am present with you both in your personal sanctification (John 17:16-23) and your corporate sanctification as a body of believers (Matthew 18:20).

You are also workmen together with Me (I Corinthians 3:9). I have a specific call to service for every believer. Not every believer has the same calling, but each has the same responsibility to serve in the place of his calling. Scripture describes three aspects of the call. Concerning its source, it is a "heavenly calling" (Hebrews 3:1). Concerning its character, it is a "holy calling" (II Timothy 1:9). Concerning its challenge, it is a call to excellence or a "high calling" (Philippians 3:14).

A final aspect of My call is one which most believers prefer to minimize—the call to suffering. Suffering is a very real part of the experience of the Christian life (cf. I Peter 2:19- 21). There are two extreme positions to be avoided in this area of the Christian life. First, some run from any and all opposition and hardship and, in doing so, often hinder My testimony and fail to learn what I am trying to teach them in their suffering. A second group seems committed to multiplying their sorrows to the same effect of hindering My testimony and at times even resisting My will when I want to bless them. Note the five areas of suffering in the Christian life in which Immanuel becomes particularly meaningful—infirmities, reproaches, necessities, persecutions, and distresses (II Corinthians 12:10).

WONDERFUL

Another of My birth names is "Wonderful." This title was first used in an appearance of the angel of the Lord to the mother of Samson (Judges 13:8-22) and later was one of the five titles Isaiah ascribed to Me the "son," "given" and the "child" "born" (Isaiah 9:6). Although many contemporary writers tend to view this Isaiah list as four compound names, the first being "Wonderful Counselor," the Hebrew word used by the prophet is a noun and not an adjective. Also, My names "Wonderful" and "Counselor" both appear independently elsewhere in Scripture as My names.

A Definition of My Wonder

This word "wonderful" is used in three different senses in the Old Testament. First, a wonder is something marvelous or spectacular. The expression "signs and wonders" is a common Old Testament designation of the miraculous. The New Testament reserves this designation for miracles of the most incredible variety. They were the kinds of miracles that left the witness with a feeling of wonder (cf. Matthew 15:31; Mark 6:51; Luke 4:22).

A second aspect of this word "wonder" is something mysterious or secret. F.C. Jennings has commented on this name of Christ: "It both expresses and hides the incomprehensible." In this way the name is closely related to the "name written, that no man knew, but he himself" (Revelation 19:12). Even when this name has been thoroughly studied, an element of mystery will still remain about all that it represents in Me.

Thirdly, that which is wonderful is separated from the common and belongs to the majestic. It falls in a class all by itself far above the common or ordinary. Charles Haddon Spurgeon suggested, "His name shall be called the separated One, the distinguished One, the noble One, set apart from the common race of mankind."

A Recognition of My Wonder

I am called "Wonderful" because I am wonderful. I am wonderful, first, in My identity. Theologians today can analyze the nature of the *kenosis*, the incarnation, and the hypostatic union of two natures, but after all is said and done, a deep mystery about My Person remains. I am wonderful, further, in My industry. Whether in My work of creation or My work of redemption, all that I did to accomplish My work was wonderful in the sense that the observer of the act or finished work feels overwhelmed with a sense of wonder. I was wonderful in My ministry to the extent that the multitudes marveled at the content of My message and the authority of My delivery.

Finally, I was wonderful in My destiny. Born in a barn on the backside of Bethlehem, the legal son of a humble carpenter, My closest associates a group of former fishermen, patriots, and traitors to their country's ideals, My humiliating death between two thieves and My hometown reputed to be "the city of garbage," I, Jesus of Nazareth, am destined someday to be declared the King of kings and Lord of lords.

A Response to My Wonder

Charles Haddon Spurgeon once announced to the great crowds who came to hear him preach, "Beloved, there are a thousand things in this world that are called by names that do not belong to them; but in entering upon my text, I must announce at the very opening, that Christ is called Wonderful, because He is so." How do you respond to that wonder?

First, you respond to My wonder with adoration. I ought to be the object of your grateful adoration and worship. Leafing through the pages of an average hymnbook will suggest dozens of suitable expressions of your adoration for Me.

Secondly, I ought to be the object of your wholehearted devotion. I alone ought to be the object of your deepest and warmest affections. The great commandment of the Law was to love Me the Lord supremely with one's total being. That also is a valid responsibility of the Christian today.

Finally, you should respond to My wonder by entering into a deeper communion with Me who is called "Wonderful." The shallow experience of many Christians today is a sad commentary on their interest in Me who loves them and gave Myself for them. If I am Wonderful, and I am, you should long to spend time with Me in Bible study and prayer and to enjoy sweet fellowship with Me in all that you do.

COUNSELOR

Another of My birth names is "Counselor." The world was brought to ruin by the counsel of the serpent in the garden of Eden. That ruined race can be restored only by Me, a counselor who advises men in the counsel of the Father. If Satan is the counselor of ruin, I am the Counselor of restoration.

The significance of My name is clear in Scripture by the fact that I Myself need no counsel (Romans 11:33,34); I am described as the fount of all wisdom and understanding (Proverbs 8:14), and is presented as imparting counsel to those who seek it (Psalms 16:7; 73:24;

Isaiah 25:1; 28:29). As you study the Scriptures, My qualifications of Counselor and the quality of My counsel become increasingly obvious. But only when you discern and apply My counsel to life do I become your Counselor.

My Qualification of Counselor

Most contemporary Christian counselors today affirm there are three basic qualifications of a biblical and effective counselor. Based upon passages such as Romans 15:14 and Colossians 3:16, they argue that the Christian counselor today must be characterized by a knowledge of the meaning of Scripture as it applies to their personal life, a goodness or empathetic concern for others, and enthusiasm for life and wisdom—that is, the skillful use of Scripture in ministry to others for My glory.

If this is what Scripture requires of a counselor, obviously, then, I excel in each and every prerequisite. One of My divine attributes is omniscience, the fullness of all knowledge. I alone am truly good. I am also the personification of the Father's wisdom. I am the Counselor par excellence, for I am the only One who fully meets the qualifications of a counselor.

The Character of My Counsel

Isaiah described My nature or character with the words "wonderful in counsel" (Isaiah 28:29). A survey of the biblical references to the counsel of the Lord indicates five aspects of its character.

First, My counsel sets controls. It controls in the sense that it guides the steps of the believer (Psalm 73:24) and establishes him in that which continues (Proverbs 11:14; 15:22; 19:21; 20:18).

Secondly, My counsel is creative. It is interesting to note how often the concept of creation stands in close proximity to a reference to Me, the Counselor (Isaiah 40:14,26; Romans 11:34,36). This is an important principle to remember. Just because your will for someone else in similar circumstances requires a certain course of action does not mean that it is My will for everyone in that same situation. You must learn to let Me be God and be creative in My counsel.

Also, My counsel comforts: "Ointment and perfume rejoice the heart: so doth the sweetness of a man's friend by hearty counsel"

(Proverbs 27:9). I in My role as Counselor am the *Paraclete* (Comforter), which the New Testament applies to Me as well as to the Holy Spirit (I John 2: 1). In both cases, one of My functions is to come alongside to help and encourage the discouraged and comfort the sorrowing.

Fourthly, My counsel is confidential. This is implied by the Greek word *sumboulos*, used by the LXX translators and New Testament writers (Proverbs 24:6; Isaiah 9:6; Romans 11:34). The term literally means "a confidential advisor." When you seek counsel from Me concerning an opportunity or problem, the resulting counsel is confidential, and you do not have to worry about later hearing the subject by the grapevine.

Finally, My counsel is corporate. In counseling the Laodicean church to anoint their eyes and improve their vision, I used the Greek verb *sumbouleuo*, meaning "to give advice jointly." The Father as the God of all comfort and the Holy Spirit as the Comforter are My other advisors to the believer. David also called the Scriptures his counselors, for they are the instrument this Trinity of counselors uses to communicate My counsel.

The Discerning of My Counsel

How can you discern My counsel in your life? Among the many principles of Scripture for discerning the will of God, five stand out predominantly. First, My counsel is revealed in the Scriptures (II Timothy 3:16,17). Secondly, My counsel often comes through prayer (Judges 20:18,23; I Samuel 14:37). Third, you discern it from the help of wise counselors (Proverbs 11:14; 12:15; 24:6). Fourth, you recognize it through circumstances. Eliezer was aware of My leading in his life, and circumstances confirmed this to be so (Genesis 15:2; 24:27). Finally, the Holy Spirit reaffirms My counsel. Paul sought to go several places to preach the gospel which were not where I wanted him to go. Because he was sensitive to the leading of the Spirit, he could discern closed doors and had a deep assurance he was doing what I wanted him to do when the doors finally opened (Acts 16:6-10).

THE MIGHTY GOD

Isaiah also called Me *El Gibbon*, "the Mighty God" (Isaiah 9:6). Although I "emptied himself" ("made Myself of no reputation"—*KJV*) to become a man (Philippians 2:7), I never abandoned My divine attributes. Is it not paradoxical that I, the Mighty God, should clothe Myself as a newborn child? If there is any question about Isaiah's view of this coming child, clearly here he indicates I am God incarnate.

Scripture used the Hebrew word *gibbon*, translated "mighty," not only of Me but also of the "mighty men" who were soldiers of Israel distinguished in battle. It conveys the idea of exceptional physical strength and prowess. When used of Me in the Old Testament, it expressed the assurance that I would defend Israel from her enemies (Psalms 24:8; 45:3). It emphasizes the attribute of omnipotence and suggests I will use that power on behalf of My people.

THE EVERLASTING FATHER

I am also called "the Everlasting Father," or more literally, "Father of Eternity." This is the most emphatic assertion of My deity offered by the prophet Isaiah. This title of Mine has caused some confusion among Christians in trying to understand the mystery of the Trinity. I am not here called the Father—as God the Father—is the Father. I am a distinct Person of the Trinity. The Persons of the Trinity are equal in nature but distinguishable in Person and distinct in duties.

The title "Father" is used here of Me in the sense of a "founding father." People will talk about the founding fathers of a country or movement, meaning those persons who were the pioneers of an idea and gave birth to the movement or nation. In this sense, I am the founding father of eternity, existing before it began and giving birth to time and history.

THE PRINCE OF PEACE

Isaiah also calls Me "the Prince of Peace." I am a Prince now and will ultimately be recognized not only as a king but as the King of kings (Revelation 19:16). As the Prince of Peace, I can meet the deepest need in the human heart—that of peace with Me, and with others round about him. Peace with Me is a result of your justification and based on My shed blood at the cross (Romans 5: 1; Ephesians 2:13; Colossians 1:20). I am both the God of Peace (Philippians 4:9) and *Jehovah Shalom* (Judges 6:24), the One who makes peace between sinners and the Father (Eph. 2:14ff).

Notice how these five names suggested by Isaiah relate to My ministry. I was Wonderful in life as I performed various signs and wonders to demonstrate who I was. I was your Counselor by example and teaching. And I perpetuated My counsel by giving you the New Testament. In My resurrection I demonstrated Myself to be the Mighty God. I ascended into glory as your Everlasting Father, and when I return, I will do so as the Prince of Peace.

CONCLUSION

When parents choose a name for their child, they often strive to select one which expresses their hopes for what the child will be someday. Parents name children after people whom they admire and respect. When the Father inspired His prophets to select names for Me—Christ Child,—the Father had the advantage of omniscience. My names not only expressed desire but affirmed the very nature and character of who I am. I am the Dayspring from on High, Immanuel, Wonderful, Counselor, the Mighty God, the Everlasting Father, and the Prince of Peace. Have you acknowledged Me to be each of these in your life?

For Discussion:

1. Of all the individuals in Scripture with supernatural births, why is My birth the greatest?
2. How am I your Dayspring?
3. How should My name and work as Immanuel affect your daily lives?
4. Name several ways Christians may express their worship of Me as "Wonderful."
5. How and when do I counsel you the believer?
6. Am I the Prince of Peace today, or is this a future event?

CHAPTER SEVEN

MY SERVICE NAMES

"Even as I, the Son of man, came not to be ministered unto, but to minister, and to give My life a ransom for many" (Matthew 20:28; Mark 10:45).

I described My ministry here on earth in terms of ministry to others. Although there were times when I was entertained by friends and others provided for My physical necessities, My primary concern was what I could do for others. Wherever I was, I found needs and met them. The crowds followed Me not so much for My dynamic charisma as for what I did for them. They came for healing, to have demons cast out, or to be fed with loaves and fish. Their motives were often less than noble. I met needs in lives, and some people chose to follow Me. I was primarily a minister to others.

When I ascended back to heaven, I continued to be a minister to others. Even today I am primarily interested in meeting the needs of people. My name represents My ability to meet a particular need in a person's life. Some people have asked, "What is My greatest name in the Scripture?" Actually, there is no standard answer to that question. The greatest name is the name that meets your greatest need. For some, it is "Jesus," My name that relates so closely to salvation. To others, it is "Christ," My name that relates so closely to victorious Christian living. Someone who is often discouraged might think of My name "Comforter" or "Consolation" as the greatest of My names.

Although every one of My names ministers to human needs, some names more characteristically describe Me in My role as minister. These names I call "My service names." There are many such names in Scripture because My range of ministry is so wide. Your objective in this chapter is to examine only a few of My more prominent service names.

When you think of My service names obviously I can serve only in the place where I am invited into your life. There are actually five aspects to My presence in Scripture. First, I am omnipresent. This means that, as God, I am at all times in every place wholly present. Then there is My localized presence, such as when Stephen saw Me standing to greet him as he was being stoned and being greeted into heaven (Acts 7:55). You can also speak of My indwelling presence; I live within the believer (Colossians 1:27). My fourth presence is My institutionalized presence. There is a sense in which I dwell in the midst of a church (Ephesians 1:22,23). Finally, I am the incarnate Word dwelling in the Scriptures, the Inspired Word. The Scriptures are, therefore, identified as the Word of Christ (Colossians 3:16).

MY CREATIVE NAMES

When you think of My service names, you must begin with those titles which relate to My creation and sustenance of this world. In this regard I am both the Creator and Sustainer of the world and all life therein. The prominent references to Me in two key Christological passages particularly emphasize this fact.

The first of these is in the first chapter of John in which I am introduced as the *Logos*. John affirmed, "All things were made by him; and without him was not anything made that was made" (John 1:3). In discussing My creative work, John uses the verb *egento*, meaning "generated or energized." I created by producing life and energy from nothing. The verse following argues, "In him was life; and the life was the light of men" (John 1:4). I am life.

The second key passage is Colossians 1:15-22. Perhaps no other statement concerning Me is as magnificent as this one. Although I am never mentioned by name in this passage, no fewer than fifteen pronouns are used to refer to Me. "For by *him* were all things created, that are in heaven, and that are in earth, visible and invisible, whether they be thrones, or dominions, or principalities, or powers: all things were created by *him*, and for *him*: and *he* is before all things, and by *him* all things consist" (Colossians 1:16,17). These verses identify Me as both the Creator and Sustainer of life. The terms "thrones, dominions, principalities, and powers" are generally considered to refer to various rankings of angels. I created them all and came before them. Here Paul is portraying Me as more than a super-angel, probably in an effort to correct a false teaching in the early church.

The word "consist" (Colossians 1:17) literally means "to hold together." This is similar to John's portrayal of Me as life. Energy is the glue that holds this universe and all of its component parts together. I am the source of energy because life begets energy. Scientists have discovered an incredible amount of energy in every atom, but I am the source of that energy. When viewing this aspect of My nature, you must be careful not to go to the extreme of Spinoza who defined energy as his god. Although I am the source of energy, you must not think of Me as energy itself.

MY INSTRUCTIVE NAMES

Several of My names in the New Testament emphasize My role as a teacher. It is interesting that the Scriptures never call Me a preacher (although that may be implied by My title Prophet). At least four terms are used to distinguish Me as a teacher. Each of these terms differs slightly in meaning, and together they give a more complete picture of both My nature and emphasis of My teaching ministry.

Rabbi

The word *rabbi* is an Aramaic word which the writers of the New Testament transliterated into the Greek. In many cases, translators have done the same, bringing the word over into the English language letter for letter. Rabbi was a common way to address a religious teacher in the first century and was first used to address Me by two of My first disciples (John 1:38). In that place John explains to his Greek readers that My title was equivalent in meaning to "Master" (*kurios*), a common Greek reference to a philosopher or teacher.

The Aramaic word literally means "my great one" and represented the great respect the Jews had for their rabbis. The title included not only the idea of teaching but also a certain content in their teaching. It was used much as we today speak of a charismatic teacher, or a deeper-life teacher, etc. When people addressed Me as "Rabbi," they were normally discerning the nature or content of My teaching.

Rabboni

The title *Rabboni* is used only on two occasions to refer to Me. It was first used by blind Bartimaeus in his request for sight (Mark 10:51). Later, Mary Magdalene used it upon her recognition of Me as the resurrected Christ. On both occasions it was used by people who had a deep sense of loyalty or affection for Me because of a major miracle I had performed in their behalf. It is an intensified form of the title "Rabbi" and might be translated "My Rabbi." When Mary used it on that resurrection morning, she no doubt spoke with deepest love for Me, the One who was not just another teacher but the One she would claim to be her own (John 20:16).

Didaskalos

A third instructive name for Me is the Greek word *didaskalos*, usually translated "teacher" or "master." This was the title Nicodemus used when he addressed Me as "a teacher come from God" (John 3:2). It was characteristic of My ministry that the crowds who heard Me teach were astonished at My doctrine or teaching (cf. Matthew 7:28,29; Mark 1:22,27). Although it is popular today to speak of My sermons, it would probably be more correct to consider them as My Adult Bible Class lessons, because they refer to My teaching rather than preaching. Six major blocks of My teaching are recorded in Matthew, including the Sermon on the Mount (Matthew 5-7), My instructions to My apostles before sending them out (Matthew 10), My parables on the kingdom of heaven (Matthew 13), My teaching on greatness in the church (Matthew 18), My sermon in the temple on the day of testing (Matthew 21-23), and the Olivet Discourse concerning things to come (Matthew 24-25). John includes an additional account of a teaching session of Mine, the Upper Room Discourse (John 13-16), and several detailed accounts of other lessons. Luke also emphasizes My teaching ministry, particularly in recording the various parables I taught.

My teaching was unique in both content and style. I taught not the tradition of men as was common in My day but the Word of God. Like the prophets of old, I spoke on behalf of God; but unlike those who prefaced their most authoritative appeals with the remark "Thus saith the Lord," I was unique for My comment, "But I say unto you." I differed from the scribes, the usual teachers of the Law, not only in content but in My style of teaching. When a scribe taught the Law, he announced his text and proceeded to recite all the various opinions of other respected teachers of the Law. Only then did he conclude by announcing the consensus of scholarship on the subject. But I spoke authoritatively with little or no appeal to the usual authorities.

Kathegetes

A final name of Mine which alludes to My teaching ministry is the term *kathegetes*, meaning "guide." It is used only on one occasion in the New Testament where I urged My disciples, "Neither be ye called masters: for one is your Master, even Christ" (Matthew 23:10). Here this term is twice translated "master" in the *King James Version*, but other translators have used words like "leader," "teacher," and "instructor" to convey the meaning of this word. It differs from the other words for "teacher" in Scripture in that it conveys the image of a teacher who influences or guides a student not only intellectually but morally. I am unique among teachers in that I alone can teach the truth and lead you most fully in the way of truth.

MY SOVEREIGN NAMES

Several different names of Mine are translated with the English word "master," including most of the instructive names cited above. But at least three of My titles include in their meaning the idea of mastery over someone or something. These too are service names of Mine, for they demonstrate My power and authority over others and, therefore, evince My ability to serve.

Epistates

Luke alone uses the Greek word *epistates*; he uses it six times of Me (Luke 5:5; 8:24–45; 9:33,49; 17:13). It is a strong term, meaning "chief, commander, leader, or overseer." It relates closely to the word translated "bishop" in the *King James Version*, which is a title of the pastor in a church (I Timothy 3:1). It designates the absolute authority of the one so addressed and would ordinarily be considered an honorable title. It was apparently never used except by a disciple and in every case occurs within a context in which the speaker's view of Me is somewhat defective. It is always followed by the user being rebuked for his action or conclusion, or the user experiencing something that causes him to grow in his understanding of who I am.

Oikodespotes

I used the term *oikodespotes* to refer to Myself in several of My parables. It is translated "master of the house" (Matthew 10:25; Luke 13:25; 14:21), "goodman of the house" (Matthew 20:11; 24:43; Mark 14:14; Luke 12:39), and "householder" (Matthew 13:27,52; 20:1; 21:33). This was the usual title for the master over the household stewards. It emphasizes the absolute control of that master over those stewards. I used this title in two contexts. First, I am master over My disciples who are stewards of the mysteries of God. Secondly, in those eschatological parables in which I used this term in the context of My return, I am master over all mankind. By this title, I claimed absolute authority over men both in this life and that to come.

Despotes

Only once am I referred to by the term *despotes* and that by Peter in his second epistle (II Peter 2:1), where the *King James Version* reads "Lord." Vine suggests this word refers to "one who has absolute ownership and uncontrolled power." It is perhaps My strongest title that argues for My Lordship. It was commonly used in Greek to refer to a master who exercised a rigid authority over his slaves and is the root of its English derivative, "despot," referring to any ruler having absolute control, particularly a tyrant or oppressive leader. The negative connotation—abuse of power—is not necessarily implied in this term, only the absolute nature of My authority.

MY ASSISTANCE NAMES

Some of My service names can best be described as "assistance names," for their primary emphasis points out how I assist the believer in living the Christian life. The Christian life has been explained as Me living in and through the Christian (cf. Galatians 2:20). Because this is true, every one of My more than 700 names and titles, in a sense, is an "assistance name." But the names considered in this section more properly belong here because of the more direct role I play in your Christian life, as implied in these names.

The Intercessor

I am your Intercessor; one of My primary works on behalf of the Christian today is that of intercession. The writer to the Hebrews noted, "Wherefore he is able also to save them to the uttermost that come unto God by him, seeing he ever liveth to make intercession for them" (Hebrews 7:25). This is one of My two primary functions as your High Priest.

The need for an intercessor has long been felt by man. In the midst of his despair, Job cried out, "O, that one might plead for a man with God, as a man pleads for his neighbor!" (Job 16:21). He realized man's greatest need was someone who could stand before a holy God on behalf of a sinful human race and pray effectively for that race. That is why he earlier lamented, "Neither is there any daysman betwixt us that might lay his hand upon us both" (Job 9:33). That missing Daysman was Me, the One whom Paul in the New Testament called "the Mediator" (I Timothy 2:5).

The twofold purpose of My Intercessor's prayer on your behalf is to keep you from sinning and, in so doing, save to the uttermost. Of My two primary ministries as your High Priest, I am concerned most with preventing problems in the Christian life. I, the Intercessor, am known for what I do; I plead that you might not sin.

The Advocate

The second of My ministries as a High Priest is advocacy. I am called "an advocate with the Father" (I John 2:1), meaning that I stand before God on your behalf. As Intercessor, I plead that you might not sin. As Advocate, I stand by you after you have sinned. John uses the Greek word *paraclete*, meaning "one called alongside to help." This is also a name of the Holy Spirit, translated in another place "Comforter" (John 16:7).

The duty of an advocate is to stand by the person and/or principles which he supports. One legal phrase used today to describe an advocate is "a friend of the court." If you have to go to court over a traffic accident, your insurance company supplies a lawyer who acts on your behalf. Throughout the course of the case, the lawyer speaks on your behalf to ensure that the court hears your side of the traffic accident. Although you do not speak in the courtroom yourself, your case is heard because of the efforts of your advocate, the lawyer.

Similarly, I act as your advocate before the Father in heaven when the devil accuses you of sin. I am the Man in the glory, a priest after the order of Melchizedek, who is both qualified and capable to represent your cause in the court of heaven. I do not actually have to plead your case every time you sin. My constant presence before the Father is the sufficient plea for your failings. My defense rests upon My work—what I accomplished at Calvary on your behalf.

Because both Intercessor and Advocate are aspects of My work as High Priest, the qualifications for both tasks are the qualifications for the priesthood. To be a priest, one needed the right birth, right calling, and right qualifications. I qualify to be your High Priest and, therefore, both your Intercessor and Advocate because, after the order of Melchizedek, I was called of God to be your High Priest and was anointed of the Holy Spirit just as priests were anointed with oil to begin their priestly ministry. The Man in the glory (Hebrews 6:19-20; 7:24) is not only your High Priest but also your Intercessor and Advocate.

The Propitiation for Your Sins

The third of My assistance names is "the Propitiation for your sins" (I John 2:1). The Greek word *hilaskomai* means "a satisfaction." It was used by pagan Greeks to describe sacrifices to their gods which were offered as an appeasement to their wrath. In the Scriptures, this word is never used in connection with any act of man that might appease the wrath of God; rather, God is propitiated by My vicarious and expiatory sacrifice. In My sacrifice on the cross, the holy and righteous character of God was vindicated, making it possible for Him to be a just God and at the same time to forgive sin. I not only accomplished the task of propitiating the Father but was Myself the propitiation or satisfaction by which God was propitiated.

John describes Me as the propitiation for your sins (plural). Earlier in this epistle he used the singular form of the noun "sin" (cf. I John 1:7-8). When the word "sin" appears as a singular noun in this epistle, the apostle is speaking of the sinful nature of man. When the noun is plural, John is speaking of the practice of sin. I not only "cleanse you from all sin" (I John 1:7) but also forgive you of your sins (I John 1:9). I am the sufficient payment or propitiation for the sins you commit—

past, present, and future—and not only for your sins "but also for the sins of the whole world" (I John 2:2). My death was sufficient to save all regardless of their history of sin.

The Indweller

Although the title "Indweller" is not found in Scripture, this name for Me is biblical in spirit. My names reflect My actions, and these acts include indwelling the believer. Many Christians realize the Holy Spirit indwells them but do not know I Myself also live within. I promised to "manifest" Myself to My disciples and later explained, "If a man love me, he will keep my words: and my Father will love him, and we will come unto him, and make our abode with him" (John 14:20-23).

The conscious recognition of My indwelling the believer is some-times called communion with Christ or the deeper Christian life. The condition which the believer must keep in order to enjoy this commu-nion is a deep love for Me which evidences itself in a willing obedience to do My commands. You cannot claim to have this kind of love for Me while you rebelliously resist the Lordship of Christ. Your obedience to the Scriptures is born not out of a legalistic spirit or fear of the con-sequences of not obeying but, rather, out of an inner desire to please Me, the One who loves you.

John uses an interesting word to describe the Father and Me mak-ing Our abode within the believer. The word *monai*, translated "abode" in John 14:23, occurs only one other time in Scripture, and there it is translated "mansions" (John 14:2). Obviously, John's use of the word here is significant. While I am in heaven preparing your mansion, you here on earth are providing Me a mansion. If I were to prepare you a mansion similar to the mansion you are preparing for Me, what would your mansion in heaven be like? When you understand that I am not only in heaven but also living within, that in itself should be an incen-tive to holy living.

CONCLUSION

I came not to be served but to serve. In many ways I am still serving you today. When you learn My service names, your appreciation of and love for Me increase. But an understanding of My service names does more for you than merely increase your love for Me. I said, "It is enough for the disciple that he be as his master" (Matthew 10:25). Since I am by name and nature a minister to the needs of others, too, you as My disciples, minister to others in My name.

For Discussion:

1. My service names which relate to My act of creation are Creator and Sustainer. Discuss each of these roles.
2. What are My instructive names? What can you learn about Me from each?
3. My sovereign names describe My role in giving direction to the believer. What can you learn about Me from each of these names?
4. My assistance names reveal how I support and help the believer. Discuss the meaning and work involved in these names.
5. Share your reaction to reviewing My service names. Which is most meaningful to you? Why?

CHAPTER EIGHT

MY SONSHIP NAMES

"I will declare the decree: the LORD hath said unto me, Thou art my Son; this day have I begotten thee" (Psalm 2:7). The Father's favorite name for Me is "Son." It is an Old Testament name (Psalm 2:7), and it has eternal implications. Christians around the world call Me "the only begotten Son." On all but one occasion I refer to God as "Father." The exception to this rule occurred when on the cross I asked, "My God, my God, why hast thou forsaken me?" (Matthew 27:46).

In John 5:19-27 I referred to Myself as "the Son" ten times in My comments to the Jews. I affirmed that I did only what I had seen the Father do (5:19), that I was the constant object of the Father's love (5:20), that the Father had and would continue to reveal all things and greater works to Me (5:20), that I had power to give life (5:21), that the Father had delegated His authority to judge to Me (5:22), that men should honor Me as they honor the Father (5:23), that those who do not honor Me offend the Father (5:23), that the Father sent Me (5:23), that the dead will rise to life when they hear My voice (5:25), that I have life in Myself (5:26), and that the Father has given to Me authority to execute judgment (5:27). Obviously, "Son" is an important title.

Of all My many names and titles, perhaps more belong to this family or category of names than to all the others. At least nineteen "sonship" names in Scripture relate to Me. These include: the Son of the Highest (Luke 1:32), the carpenter's son (Matthew 13:55), the son of Mary (Mark 6:3), the son of David (Mark 10:47), the son of Joseph (John 1:45), Son (Matthew 11:27), his Son from Heaven (I Thessalonians 1:10), My beloved Son (Matthew 3:17), the Son of God (John

1:49), the son of Abraham (Matthew 1:1), the Son of man (John 1:51), the Son of the Blessed (Mark 14:61), the Son of the Father (II John 3), the Son of the freewoman (Galatians 4:30), the Son of the living God (Matthew 16:16), the Son of the most high (Mark 5:7), a son over his own house (Hebrews 3:6), the Son who is consecrated for evermore (Hebrews 7:28), and the only begotten Son (John 3:16).

Although each of My nineteen "sonship names" possesses a special and important significance, this chapter will examine only three of the more prominent names. Each of these three names is used in John 3 in connection with My meeting with Nicodemus. Note the phrases "Son of man" (John 3:14), referring to My Messianic office and humanity; "only begotten Son" (3:16), referring to My unique relation to God; and "Son of God" (3:18), having special reference to My divine nature and character.

SON OF MAN

"Son of man" is particularly noteworthy because in the Gospels it appears to be My favorite title for Myself. I never identified Myself as "Jesus" until I appeared to Paul on the Damascus Road and then only one other time to the Apostle John fifty years later (Revelation 22:16). Only once did I call Myself Lord, and that was in quoting from the Old Testament (Matthew 22:43). Over eighty times during My three-and-a-half-year ministry, I called Myself "the Son of man." It is also interesting to note that only I used this term and that no one else ever addressed Me as "the Son of man."

Why was this term My favorite title for Myself? The answer to this question lies in its biblical background. The only occurrence of the term in the Old Testament with any significance appears in Daniel 7:13. There it is a title of Messianic expectation. Daniel describes Me in the context of My return and kingdom. This is the only use of the expression in the Old Testament in which it refers to Me. Other occurrences of the term in the Old Testament have a different sense (cf. Ezekiel 2:1,3,8; 3:1; 4:1; etc.).

Daniel's vision contrasts My kingdom with the succession of world empires symbolically represented as the lion (Babylon), the bear (Medo-Persia), the leopard (Greece), and the fourth beast—described only as "dreadful and terrible" (Rome). When these great powers and kingdoms pass, I "like the Son of man" remain (Daniel 7:13-14). Closely associated with Me are a dominion, glory, and a kingdom which are greater than all that had come before. The Jews expected their Messiah to conquer an existing kingdom (that is, Rome). They refused My Messianic claims when I did not fulfill their preconceived notions about what Messiah must be like and must do. But someday I will receive the kingdoms of the world from God the Father. I will claim them as King of kings and Lord of lords. This aspect of the prophecy still awaits fulfillment.

The context of John 3 suggests a second reason why I may have favored this name over others: "And no man hath ascended up to heaven, but he that came down from heaven, even the Son of man which is in heaven" (John 3:13). When I was born in Bethlehem, I acquired something I had never possessed before—a human nature. Although I remained God, I became also a man; I possessed a complete human nature. Because I wanted to identify with those I came to save, I chose to call Myself "the Son of man." The key verse of the Gospel of Luke affirms, "For the Son of man is come to seek and to save that which was lost" (Luke 19:10).

I referred to Myself as Son of man in three contexts. I was, first, the Son of man in the context of My earthly ministry (cf. Matthew 8:20; 9:6; 11:19; 16:13; Luke 19:10; 22:48). Secondly, I used this title also when describing My approaching death on the cross (cf. Matthew 12:40; 17:9,22; 20:18; Mark 10:33; Luke 9:22; John 3:14; 8:28; 12:23; 13:31). Finally, I used this title in an eschatological context with reference to My second coming (Matthew 13:41; 24:27,30; 25:31; Luke 18:8; 21:36).

THE ONLY BEGOTTEN SON

When someone asked a little boy what he learned in Sunday school, he replied that the lesson was on "God's Only Forgotten Son." He went on to explain how people forgot about Him, and He had to be born in a stable, and later His parents forgot about Him and left Him in the temple. Although the little boy had misheard the title "Only Begotten Son," he was also right about "God's Only Forgotten Son." People today still forget Me as was also common during My life (cf. John 1:10-12).

The name "only begotten Son" (John 3:16) did not originate in the Gospels but, rather, in heaven before time began. In the first of the Messianic Psalms, David noted, "I will declare the decree: the Lord hath said unto me, Thou art my Son; this day have I begotten thee" (Psalm 2:7). Over the years, several suggestions have been offered as to the "day" in which I was begotten. In order to resolve a doctrinal controversy in the early church, the church fathers coined the expression "eternal generation." When they speak of the eternal generation of the Son, they mean that I was eternally the Son and did not become the Son at My birth, baptism, death, resurrection, ascension, or at any other historical point in My incarnate life. If I became the Son at a point in time, I would not be the eternal Son and, therefore, not related to the Father as the Son from eternity.

You should understand the difference between being begotten and being identified or named as a son. Traditionally, Jews name their sons eight days after birth, at the time of their circumcision. It is not, therefore, unusual that a period of time should exist between the eternal generation of the Son and various times when I was named or called the Son. Elmer Towns had only one begotten son. When his son was born May 8, 1956, they named him Stephen Richard Towns.

About ten years later, he heard another man calling his son by several terms of endearment that sounded too effeminate to belong to a boy. Turning to Stephen, he said, "If I ever give you a nickname, it is not going to be something effeminate like that boy is called. I would call you something strong, like 'Sam,' a real man's name." For some reason, the name stuck, and to this day, even though he is now deceased, his son is still referred to in memory as Sam Towns. He was begotten Stephen Richard Towns in 1956 but called "Sam" in 1966. Similarly, I was called the Son at My birth, baptism, death, resurrection, and ascension, but I was begotten as Son in eternity past.

Two different Hebrew words for "Son" are used in Psalm 2: *ben* and *bar*. Each has its own distinctive meaning, although both are used throughout the Scriptures to identify the male descendant of a father. The first word, *ben* (2:7), refers to that which I achieve—that is, My Lordship. As the firstborn, I am the builder of God's spiritual house. The second word, *bar* (2:12), refers to that which I receive as heir of all things—that is, My legacy. The first refers to My honor; the latter, to My heritage.

The word "begotten" emphasizes My uniqueness. All who receive Me by faith are "sons of God" but not in the same sense that I am the only begotten Son (cf. John 1:12). God had only one Son, and He sent Me to be a missionary. To Me He gave the promise, "Ask of me, and I shall give thee the heathen for thine inheritance, and the uttermost parts of the earth for thy possession" (Psalm 2:8).

This phrase "only begotten Son" occurs on three other occasions in the Gospel of John. John beheld "the glory as of the only begotten of the Father" (1:14), noted "the only begotten Son, which is in the bosom of the Father" (1:18), and later identified Me as "the only begotten Son of God" (3:18). My uniqueness is alluded to prophetically in a birth name given to Me by Isaiah when he distinguished between "a child is born" and "a son is given" (Isaiah 9:6). I had both a human nature (a child born) and a divine nature (a son given). Neither nature in any way hindered or altered the other nature. I am the God-man—one Person with two natures. "Generation" and "only begotten" are the terms which best express the eternal relationship that existed between Me, the divine Person, and the divine Person of the Father.

THE SON OF GOD

The Gospel of John primarily purposes to produce faith in the reader, more specifically, "that ye might believe that Jesus is the Christ, the Son of God; and that believing ye might have life through his name" (John 20:31). It may be frustrating when you hear or read the arguments of liberals who note My use of the name "Son of man" and insist that I never claimed to be God, only man. It is only when you fully understand My humanity that you see My deity. Likewise, only when you fully see My deity can you then see My humanity.

Although some people like to distinguish between the expressions "God the Son" and "Son of God," the difference is more imagined than real. The phrase "son of" was a common Hebraism to denote a relationship in which the "son" possessed the very same nature as that of which he was "son." Even today, the highest honor a Jew can receive is to be recognized as "a son of Israel" by the Israeli government, meaning that he is by nature the personification of the true spirit of the nation. The expression "Son of God," therefore, means I am by nature the personification of God Himself: I am the very same essence as the Father.

When you refer to Me as "the Son of God," you do not mean that I am in any way inferior to or less than God the Father. In every respect the name "Son of God" implies that I am both co-equal and co-eternal with the Father. This is also true of other forms of this name—such as, "Son of the Blessed" (Mark 14:61), "the Son of the Father" (II John 3), "the Son of the Highest" (Luke 1:32), "the Son of the living God" (Matthew 16:16), and "Son of the most high" (Mark 5:7).

My relationship to the Father was not something that I discovered only later in life. As a twelve-year-old boy, I understood I was the Son of God and needed to be about My Father's business (Luke 2:49). This was also reaffirmed at My baptism. When I was dipped into the water by John the Baptist, God the Father "thundered" from heaven, "Thou art my beloved Son, in whom I am well pleased" (Mark 1:11). When I was tempted by Satan, I did not dispute that I was indeed the Son of God (Luke 4:3,9), and Satan knew full well that I was the Son of God.

I later encountered a demon-possessed person who called Me "Son of the most high God" (Mark 5:7). "God Most High" (*El Elyon*) is the name of God which demons most often used. Satan fell from his exalted position when he attempted to be like *El Elyon* (Isaiah 14:14). Melchisedek used this name to identify the Possessor of heaven and earth (Genesis 14:19). The constant attack of Satan against *El Elyon* often takes the form of destroying or taking possession of that which rightfully belongs to God.

At My trial, I was accused and charged with both insurrection (at the Roman trials) and blasphemy (at the Jewish trials). I was asked by the high priest, "I adjure thee by the living God, that thou tell us whether thou be the Christ, the Son of God" (Matthew 26:63). While I hung on the cross, My enemies mocked Me with statements such as, "If thou be the Son of God, come down from the cross" (Matthew 27:40); and, "He trusted in God; let him deliver him now, if he will have him: for he said, I am the Son of God" (Matthew 27:43).

CONCLUSION

I am not only the Son of man but also the only begotten Son of God. That is what I claimed and taught. That being the case, you must respond to Me in one of three ways. If I lied about My identity and knew it, then My attempt at deception was such that I got exactly what

I deserved. If I believed I was the Son of God and deceived Myself, then I should be regarded not as a liar but, rather, as a lunatic on the level of a man who thinks he is Napoleon. If, however, I was telling the truth—that is, if I really am the Son of God that I claimed to be—then you must recognize and worship Me as none other than the Lord of life and very God of very God. My claim to be the Son of God gives you these three alternatives today. You must all answer the haunting question of Pilate, "What shall I do then with Jesus which is called Christ?" (Matthew 27:22).

For Discussion:

1. Giving Me the title Son implies that the first Person of the Trinity is the Father. What do the sonship names reveal about the Trinity?
2. There are 19 sonship titles. Which three are predominant? Why?
3. Of all My names, which one did I use most frequently in reference to Myself? Why do you think I preferred this name?
4. Why was I called the only begotten Son?
5. The title Son of God reminds you of My deity. Can a person be saved apart from belief in My deity? Why or why not?

CHAPTER NINE

MY GODHEAD NAMES

"And Simon Peter answered and said, Thou art the Christ, the Son of the living God" (Matthew 16:16).

Several of My names are commentaries on My character, My nature, and My attributes. For a complete understanding of who I am, you should consider all of My names, but certain names are foundational to My divine nature. Usually these names appear in the context of an important Christological passage of Scripture or stress some unique aspect or attribute of Me and/or My relationship to the Godhead. These names describe Me as God incarnate, "the Christ of God" (Luke 9:20).

I AM THE WORD

The Apostle John was exclusive in calling Me by the title "Word." Using the Greek word *logos*, John wrote, "In the beginning was the Word, and the Word was with God, and the Word was God" (John 1:1). He also began his first epistle with a variation of this title. There he noted, "That which was from the beginning, which we have heard, which we have seen with our eyes, which we have looked upon, and our hands have handled, of the Word of life" (I John 1:1). The apostle also used a form of the title in describing My return to this earth: "And he was clothed with a vesture dipped in blood; and his name is called The Word of God" (Revelation 19:13).

Words are indispensable to language. You use them to communicate a message. Without them you could not explain precisely what you mean. A word defines or describes the idea you intend to pass on to others. When the Jews used the word *logos*, they thought in terms of the Wisdom literature of the Old Testament.

Scholars debate whether John borrowed the term *logos* from the Greeks or the Jews. If the term is Greek, there may be numerous philosophical implications. If the term is Hebrew, John may be making reference to the wisdom of God personified (Proverbs, especially chapters 5-8). Probably John calls Me "the Word of God" because this phrase is used over 1200 times in the Old Testament to refer to the revelation or message of God, as in the phrase, "the Word of God came to." I am the message communicated from God the Father to mankind. I am the personification of everything the written and spoken Word of the Lord was in the Old Testament. I am, therefore, the expression, revelation, and communication of the Lord. I am both the incarnate and inspired Word. The following listing summarizes the primary ideas of John's introduction concerning the Word:

TEN CONCLUSIONS ABOUT THE WORD IN JOHN 1:1-18

1. The phrase "In the beginning" is not a reference to a point in time but a reference to eternity past (1:1.).

2. The personality of the Word is evident in that it is capable of individualization (1:1).

3. The Word has active and personal communication with God the Father (1:1,2).

4. There are two centers of consciousness, for I, the Word, was God yet also I was "face to face" with God the Father (1:1).

5. The Word has the essence of deity (1:1).

6. The Father and the Word are one (1:1).

7. The Word was the Agent by which God expressed or revealed Himself (1:18).

8. The incarnate Word has a definite continuity with the preincarnate Word (1:1,14).

9. As God the Father lived in a tent, spoke in a tent, and revealed Himself in the Old Testament tabernacle, so I, the Word, tabernacled among people (1:14).

10. The incarnation of the Word is the unique revelation of God (1:4).

I AM THE BELOVED

The title "Beloved" occurs only once in Scripture (Ephesians 1:6), although many passages affirm the Father's love for Me. God called Me "my beloved Son" at My baptism (Matthew 3:17), and I repeatedly acknowledged that "the Father loves the Son" (John 3:35; 5:20; 17:23). Paul notes you are "accepted in the beloved" (Ephesians 1:6). The particularly comforting aspect of this title is the context in which it is revealed. I am the object of the Father's love, and because you are in Me, you too are the object of the Father's love.

I AM THE IMAGE OF GOD

The Greek word *eikon*, meaning "image," is twice used in My titles to express My unique relation to God the Father. The word itself denotes an image and involves the two ideas of representation and manifestation. When Paul affirmed that I am "the image of God" (II Corinthians 4:4), he meant I was essentially and absolutely the perfect representation and manifestation or expression of the Father. In another place Paul altered the title slightly by calling Me "the image of the invisible God" (Colossians 1:15). This emphasized that I am the visible representation and manifestation of God the Father to created beings. Both contexts convey the idea of perfection in that image.

A second closely related title is "the express image of his person" (Hebrews 1:3). This is one of seven such statements in the early verses of Hebrews—all designed to demonstrate My superiority. Various versions translate it in different ways: "the very image of his substance" (*ASV*), "an exact representation of his very being" (*Rhm*), "flawless expression of the nature of God" (*Phillips*), "stamped with God's own character" (*Moffat*), "the copy of his being" (*Beck*), "the exact representation of God's nature" (*Swindoll*), "the exact expression of God's nature" (*Stibbs*), "the impress of the Divine Nature" (*F.B. Meyer*), and "the exact expression of God's very essence" (*Barclay*). This wide assortment of translations derives from two key Greek words in this title.

The first of these is the word character, which is closely related to the verb *charasso*, meaning "to cut, to scratch, or to mark." Originally this word referred to a marking agent, such as a die, and then later to the impression made by the marking agent. It is similar to the English word "stamp," which first referred to the instrument which printed the impression and later to the impression itself. It suggests the idea of an exact representation of the person or the person himself—that is, the distinguishing features or traits by which a person or thing is known (cf. the English word "characteristics"). What the writer of Hebrews seems to argue by using this title is that as the wax bears the impression of the seal pressed upon it, revealing all the dominant character traits of that seal, even so I bear the impression of God's essential being, revealing all the attributes of God.

The second word in this title is *hypostasis*, which is more of a philosophical than a theological term. Etymologically, it refers to the sediment or foundation under a building but came to be used by Greek philosophers to refer to the essence or real being of a person thought to rest under the surface appearance of the person. It refers to the substance of what you are. Used here of Me in this context, it is an argument for My deity, for I am substantially God.

ATTRIBUTIVE NAMES

Several of My character names may be classed as attributive names, for in their meaning they focus upon the various attributes of God. These names underscore two of the more prominent attributes—holiness and righteousness.

In several passages I am called the Holy One. The child to be born to Mary was "that holy thing" (Luke 1:35); later the apostles called Me "thy holy child Jesus" (Acts 4:30). On several occasions the apostles referred to Me as the "Holy One" (Acts 2:27; 13:36; cf. Psalm 89:18). The primary thought in these designations is that of consecration or being set apart uniquely unto God. My holiness is a fundamental requirement of the worthy sacrifice for sin. Because of My holiness, you become holy. One of the biblical titles for the Christian is "saint," which is connected in thought to the idea of holiness.

Righteousness also is a feature in several of My names and titles. I am called "the righteous" (II John 2:1), "a righteous Branch" (Jeremiah 23:5), "the righteous LORD" (Psalm 11:7), "my righteous servant" (Isaiah 53:11), "the righteous judge" (II Timothy 4:8), "a righteous man" (Luke 23:47), "righteousness" (I Corinthians 1:30), and "the righteousness of God" (Romans 10:3). As holiness refers primarily to My character, so righteousness refers primarily to My conduct. These two titles are closely related because it is impossible to be righteous without being holy. My righteousness is an expression of My holiness just as righteousness is the spontaneous expression of the saint.

My holiness and righteousness are best expressed in My sinlessness. My sinlessness is like a four-legged chair, because there are four Scriptures that affirm I "knew no sin" (II Corinthians 5:21), "did no sin" (I Peter 2:22), was "without sin" (Hebrews 4:15), and could not be convicted of sin (John 8:46). Just as a four-legged chair is the most secure in which to sit, these four statements serve to affirm My sinless perfection.

PRIORITY NAMES

Several of My names and titles may be called "priority names," for they emphasize My priority either in My Person or accomplishment. The Apostle Paul emphasized this concept when he noted "that in all things he might have the preeminence" (Colossians 1:18). Each of the following names refers to Me in this sense.

I am called "mine elect" (Isaiah 42:1) or "the chosen of God" (Luke 23:35). This title emphasizes My priority as the uniquely appointed Servant of the Lord. When you have a job that needs to be done, often you will spend time looking for the most qualified one to accomplish the task. The greater the job, the more diligently you seek out the most capable and qualified person available. You want to be sure that the chosen one is the best available. When God sought to redeem a lost world, only I qualified to successfully complete that task, and God the Father chose Me to do it. When the mockers at the foot of the cross called out to Me as "the chosen of God" (Luke 23:35), they no doubt were adding insults to My suffering.

Actually, it was a reminder to Me who at any moment could have called on legions of angels to release Me and destroy My enemies that I was God's Elect, chosen to complete the specific task in which I was then engaged.

Several of My titles include the words, "the firstborn" (Hebrews 12:23). I am "the firstborn among many brethren" (Romans 8:29), "the firstborn of the dead" (Revelation 1:5, "first begotten" in *KJV*), "the firstborn of every creature" (Colossians 1:15), and the "firstborn son" (Luke 2:7). The emphasis of the Greek word *prototokos*, translated "firstborn" or "first-begotten" in Scripture, is My priority in relationships. When used of Me, it affirms My priority with the Father and preeminence over all creation. It does not imply the idea that I first came into existence at some point of time, rather, it is used in the sense that I held a certain superiority of position (cf. Exodus 4:22; Deuteronomy 21:16,17).

Another of My priority names relates to the concept of firstfruits (Romans 11:16; I Corinthians 15:20). The Greek word *aparche* closely relates to the verb *aparchomai*, meaning "to make a beginning," and was normally used in Scripture in the context of the offering of the first part of the harvest. As My title, it is a guarantee of your resurrection after the pattern of My resurrection. Just as the firstfruits of the harvest assure the farmer that more will follow, so My resurrection assures you of your future resurrection.

I AM CHRIST YOUR PASSOVER

The Apostle Paul urged the church at Corinth to deal with sin in their personal and corporate lives, stating, "Purge out therefore the old leaven, that ye may be a new lump, as ye are unleavened. For even Christ our passover is sacrificed for us" (I Corinthians 5:7). Although I am the fulfillment of all of Israel's typical feasts and sacrifices, the need for personal holiness in Corinth caused the apostle to single out the passover and apply this word to Me.

The passover feast was so named because of the promise of Father which accompanied its first observance, "And the blood shall be to you for a token upon the houses where ye are: and when I see the blood, I will pass over you, and the plague shall not be upon you to destroy you, when I smite the land of Egypt" (Exodus 12:13). The final of the ten plagues in the land of Egypt involved the death of the firstborn son in every home. Israel was instructed to kill a lamb as a substitutionary sacrifice and apply that blood to the doorpost of the home. By midnight "there was not a house where there was not one dead" (Exodus 12:30). In the homes stained with blood, the lamb was dead. In the homes lacking the bloodstain, the firstborn son of the family was dead.

Sin is destructive and deserving of the death sentence, but I, your Passover, have died in your place. Because of this, you are spared the inevitable consequences of sin. But when you understand My title and the work it emphasizes, your natural response is to look inward and begin the process of purging yourselves of sinful attitudes and habits that are a part of your being. To effect this response in you, I have given you the Holy Spirit. The fact that some things which are wrong in your life still bother you is an evidence of the work of the Holy Spirit in reminding you of the real nature of sin.

I AM THE ALPHA AND OMEGA

It is impossible for finite language to describe exhaustively the meaning of My Person and work in a single title or name, but if one comes close, it is the title "Alpha and Omega" (Revelation 1:8). Two other related titles are "the first and the last" (Revelation 1:17) and "the beginning and the ending" (Revelation 1:8). These names are significant not so much for what they say as what they imply. Alpha is the first or beginning letter of the Greek alphabet. Omega is the last or ending letter of the same. The expression should not, however, be limited only to the literal first and last letters of the alphabet, for the expressions were used much as today you speak of "everything from A to Z."

I am everything from the first to the last, the beginning to the ending, the alpha to the omega, A to Z. I am, as the apostle put it, "all, and in all" (Colossians 3:11). These related titles serve to emphasize My inexhaustibility. What do I mean to you? Perhaps you have passed through a particular experience in which I met an unusual need in your life. Even if you cannot find a specific name or title in Scripture to express adequately what happened to you, it is covered under these expressions. Before going on in this book, pause again and turn to the back of the book and review each of the more than 700 of My names in Scripture. I am all of these and more. One name cannot express all that I am, and over 700 names cannot exhaust what I am.

CONCLUSION

On the day Peter affirmed that I was the Christ of God, he probably did not comprehend all that was involved in My character. I am uniquely related to My Father as the Beloved and the eternal Word, who was face-to-face with God in eternity past. I am the One whose names suggest the very attributes of God. I am the One who holds preeminence in all things and priority before all. I am God Himself, the express image of the Father's Person, and the visible image of the invisible God.

But in the experience of the believer I am even more than that. I am Christ your Passover, the One who died in your place in order to redeem you from the infection of sin. In fact, I am everything to the child of God. I am the Alpha and Omega, the First and the Last, the Beginning and the Ending, and everything in between.

For Discussion:

1. Why am I called the Word? What does this indicate about My character and work?
2. What does "accepted in the beloved" (Ephesians 1:6) mean?
3. As the Image of God, what do I reflect? How does this name relate to believers?
4. Several of My names come from the attributes of God. Discuss how each of these names reflects a different aspect of God's nature.
5. Does the title Firstborn imply that I came into existence at some point in time? Why or why not?
6. As the Passover, what do I for the believer?
7. I am the Alpha and Omega. I am the beginning and ending of what? In light of this truth, how should you view your trials and struggles?

CHAPTER TEN

MY JEHOVISTIC TITLES

"Jesus said unto them, Verily, verily, I say unto you, Before Abraham was, I am" (John 8:58).

The Bible records many statements concerning My deity, but perhaps none were so impressive to the early church as those which identified Me with Jehovah in the Old Testament. Although the name "Jehovah" was used before the time of Moses, it was not until then that I revealed the uniqueness of My meaning (Exodus 6:3). Jehovah was My covenant name in the Old Testament and a form of the verb "to be" repeated twice. When Moses maintained he did not know My name, I revealed My name as "I AM THAT I AM" (Exodus 3:14). The name Jehovah is the I AM. This name is printed in the English Bible by the title "LORD," in which all four letters are capitalized.

"Jehovah" was My most respected name in the Old Testament. When some scribes were copying the Scriptures and came to this name, they would change their clothes and find a new pen and fresh ink to write the name. They refused even to pronounce the name as they read the Scriptures; they substituted the name *Adonai* for it. As a result of this misguided expression of reverence, considerable debate has arisen over the actual pronunciation of the name. Although most conservative theologians argue it should be pronounced Je-hov-ah, many liberal teachers argue it should be pronounced Yah-weh. It is impossible to resolve this debate now at a time when the name has remained unpronounced for generations. Even if the Hebrew language included vowels, your task of deciding about how to pronounce this name would be difficult. Dialects change within languages over years of use, so that the same word pronounced one way today may sound totally different two hundred years from today. If you did not know the history of the region, it would be hard for you to believe that the original settlers of the Southeastern United States spoke English with a thick British accent. Over the years and generations since they first settled, they have developed their own unique dialect of English. The same thing no doubt happened to the Hebrew language over a long period.

I used the expression "I am" in eight contexts within the Gospel of John, revealing something about My character as Jehovah. The Greek words which John used on those occasions, *ego eimi*, emphatically drew attention to their significance. The following listing identifies the eight contexts in which I called Myself "I AM" and is the group of names which this chapter discusses:

MY JEHOVISTIC NAMES IN THE GOSPEL OF JOHN

1. I AM the Bread of Life .... John 6:35
2. I AM the Light of the World .... John 8:12
3. I AM the Door .... John 10:9
4. I AM the Good Shepherd .... John 10:11
5. I AM the Resurrection and the Life .... John 11:25
6. I AM the Way, the Truth, and the Life.... John 14:6
7. I AM the True Vine .... John 15:1,5
8. I AM...I AM... John 4:26; 8:58; 18:5,6,8

I AM THE BREAD OF LIFE

The Jews widely believed they would recognize the Messiah because I would find the lost ark of the covenant hidden by Jeremiah and produce the jar of manna hidden therein. Hence, Messiah would be identified with manna or bread. Also, the Jews thought that being a Prophet like unto Moses (Deuteronomy 18:15) meant I would produce the bread from heaven. One rabbinical saying declared, "As was the first redeemer, so was the final redeemer; as the first redeemer caused the manna to fall from heaven, even so shall the second redeemer will cause the manna to fall." Further the Jews thought that manna would be the food in the kingdom of God. In the Jewish mind, manna excited Messianic expectations.

In light of this cultural context, it is not surprising that those who were one day ready to declare Me to be the Messiah should the next day raise the subject of manna. Twice in a meeting with Me, they requested that I produce this manna (John 6:30-31,34). In response, I identified Myself as the manna when I declared, "I am the bread of life" (John 6:35). In the discourse in which I revealed this Jehovistic title, I explained I was the bread of everlasting life (John 6:32-34), the bread of satisfying life (John 6:35-36), the bread of resurrection life (John 6:37-47), and the bread of indwelling life (John 6:48-59).

Just as a person eats bread to sustain his physical life, so the Christian must "eat" the Bread of Life to sustain his spiritual life. In My address on the Bread of Life, I used two different verbs for eating, showing two responses to the Bread. First, I used the verb *phagein*, always in an aorist tense and with reference to eternal life (John 6:50,51,52,53). When a person receives Me as Savior, he is, in this context, "eating his flesh." This is a reference to "once-and-for-all" salvation. The second verb, *trogon* (to eat), is a present active participle, which emphasizes a continual or habitual eating. It was used of munching on fruit, vegetables, or cereals. The change in tense which accompanies the change in verb emphasizes the continual satisfying of a spiritual appetite through constantly or habitually munching on the Bread of Life (John 6:54,56,57,58). If the first act of once-and-for-all eating speaks of your salvation, the second speaks of constant munching in uninterrupted communion with Me.

I AM THE LIGHT OF THE WORLD

On several occasions the religious leaders in Jerusalem tried to destroy Me. One attempt involved bringing to Me a woman caught in the act of adultery and calling on Me to pass judgment. It created for Me what they thought was an impossible situation. If I condemned her as required by the Law, the people would be disappointed and stop following Me. If I failed to uphold the Law, I was guilty of teaching contrary to Moses and could be thrown out of the Synagogue and stoned for blasphemy. I upheld the Law in its true spirit by bringing conviction to the woman's accusers and salvation to the guilty woman. At the same time I increased My already growing popularity with the common people.

Immediately following that incident, I announced, "I am the light of the world" (John 8:12). That simple statement was rich in meaning in the context in which it occurs in this Gospel. I uttered it in the court of the women, where I had been teaching. At that place were located the four golden candelabra, each with four golden bowls. As part of the previous week's celebration of the Feast of Tabernacles, these bowls had been filled with oil and lighted. Contemporary observers affirmed that the light was so brilliant it illuminated the entire city of Jerusalem. Those who gathered around Me that morning would no doubt still remember the spectacle of the night before.

By calling Myself "the light of the world," I may have been alluding to the cloud/pillar of fire that led Israel through the wilderness. The ceremonial illumination of a temple was a reminder to the people of that cloud/pillar. Most Jews would have considered that phenomenon a theophany, a manifestation of God Himself. If I was thinking of this background, then My claim to be the Light of the World is a clear title to deity.

I may also have been referring to the rising of the sun. I had begun teaching very early in the morning—that is, just before sunrise (John 8:2). By the time I made this claim, the sun would be bursting over the horizon. Because of the mountainous terrain, the sunrise in Palestine is sudden and spectacular. Within an hour, the degree of light changes from the darkest hour of the night to the brilliance of the day. It was this unique sunrise which caused David to compare the sun to "a bridegroom coming out of his chamber" (Psalm 19:5).

Another possible context to better understand My statement about being the light of the world is that of the Old Testament prophecies associated the coming of the Messiah with light. On the preceding day, Nicodemus' colleagues in the Sanhedrin had mildly rebuked him with the statement, "Search, and look: for out of Galilee arises no prophet" (John 7:52). I called Myself "the light of the world" in order to remind these Jewish leaders of very important prophecies they seemed to have forgotten (Isaiah 9:1; 42:6; 49:6; 60:1-3; Malachi 4:2). These prophecies specifically named Galilee as the place in which Messianic light would particularly shine.

One other context clarifies the sense in which I am uniquely the Light of the World. I am the light that repels the sinner who will not repent of his sin but at the same time, attracts those sinners who will. In the confrontation prior to this statement, I spoke to bring conviction to the self-righteous Jewish leaders who had sought to exploit the woman caught in the act of adultery. The word John uses in this context for "convicted" is *elegchomenoi*, literally meaning "to bring to the light and expose" (John 8:9). It describes the act of holding a letter to a lamp to see what was inside. I am the Light of the World in the sense that I hold up lives of people to the light to expose the sin hidden deep within. When I convict of sin and men are not willing to repent, they cannot remain in the light of My presence. Many people today are trying to run from God because they are convicted of some sin for which they will not repent.

I am the Light of the World, and one of the primary functions of light is to shine to reveal what was otherwise hidden. I shine to reveal Myself (John 8:12-20), the Father (John 8:21-27), and the cross (John 8:28-30). I not only expose the hidden sin in man but show him how the sin problem can be ultimately resolved. I am the light in a world of moral darkness.

I AM THE DOOR

When I identified Myself as the door, I was comparing Myself to the purpose or function of a door (John 10:9). A door was the means by which the sheep entered into the fold. By way of application, I am the door to the fold of salvation. In this context, I emphasize the exclusiveness of Myself as Savior by using the definite article "the" and by identifying salvation exclusively with entering into the fold through that door. The Greek expression *di'emou* ("by me") stands in an emphatic position so as to identify clearly the door by which individuals may find salvation.

There are at least three specific applications of this particular title in the Christian life. "I am the door: by me if any man enter in, he shall be saved, and shall go in and out, and find pasture" (John 10:9). First, I the Door, provide salvation when you enter. Secondly, you have liberty to go in and out—in for salvation and out for service. Thirdly, you shall find spiritual food in Me.

I AM THE GOOD SHEPHERD

I twice identified Myself as "the good shepherd" (John 10:11,14). In doing so, I used the Greek word *kalos*, "for good," which carried with it certain moral overtones. In classical Greek, these words were used to describe that which was beautiful, useful, auspicious, noble, wholesome, competent, and morally good. It would be correct to use any or all of these adjectives to describe Me, the Good Shepherd. This word emphasizes My essential goodness as the Shepherd which, because it is evident to the observer, results in My being admired, respected, and loved by others.

Many commentators believe this title is a reference to Jehovah Rohi of the Twenty-Third Psalm. The primary emphasis of the title, however, is My (Shepherd's) giving My life for My sheep and, therefore, is probably better understood within the context of Psalm 22, the first of the trilogy of Shepherd Psalms (Psalms 22-24). The title "Shepherd" was a church name, for Scripture occasionally identifies the church as the flock of God (I Peter 5:2).

I AM THE RESURRECTION AND THE LIFE

When I met with Martha just prior to the raising of her brother Lazarus from the dead, I introduced another of My Jehovistic names. "Jesus said unto her, I am the resurrection, and the life: he that believes in me, though he were dead, yet shall he live: And whosoever liveth and believes in me shall never die" (John 11:25,26). Martha had expressed her faith in the resurrection as a principle, but I revealed to her the resurrection as a Person, that Person being Myself. One of My titles is "Life," and I am the resurrection because I am life in its fullest sense.

This title carries with it a twofold promise for the believer. First, those who have experienced physical death shall rise to immortality. Second, none who believe shall be hurt in the second death. Although you commonly hear this title "Life" at funerals where these promises are repeated, they are conditional promises, and this name has meaning and benefit only to those who believe.

I AM THE WAY, THE TRUTH, AND THE LIFE

Alone with My disciples on the last night before the end of My life here on earth, I revealed two additional Jehovistic titles. The first of these is "the way, the truth, and the life" (John 14:6). The Greek word *hados* literally means "road" or "highway." In the context of the language of a journey, I am the highway to heaven. Further, I am the only highway to heaven. The New Testament consistently teaches an exclusiveness with respect to Me as the only Savior. I claimed to be the only Savior (John 14:6), and the disciples acknowledged it also (Acts 4:12). This description of Me was so characteristic of the nature of New Testament Christianity that My followers were described as being "of the way" or "this way" (Acts 9:2; 19:23; 22:4; 24:14,22).

I was not only the way but also the truth in its most absolute nature. I am the fountain and standard of truth. This was important to the Jews. One Jewish legend reports a group of rabbis were praying in order to determine the essential nature of God when God sent a scroll down from heaven with the first, middle, and last letters of the Hebrew alphabet on it. These three letters spell the Hebrew word for "truth." Although the story is no doubt apocryphal, it does serve to illustrate the importance of truth to the Jews, especially as an attribute of God.

And I am the life. I am unique among men in that I have life in Myself. I am described in the context of My resurrection as a "quickening" or life-giving spirit (I Corinthians 15:45). Life is fundamental to My being and is described early in the fourth Gospel as the life which was the light of all men (John 1:4).

I AM THE TRUE VINE

The second Jehovistic title I revealed that night in the Upper Room was "I am the Vine" (John 15:1,5). Vineyards were so plenteous in Israel that the vine became a national symbol. A golden vine had been engraved over the temple-gate area, and it had been used on coins minted during the Maccabean revolt. Throughout the Old Testament, a vine had been used to describe the nation (Psalm 80:8; Isaiah 5:1-7; Jeremiah 2:21; Ezekiel 15; 19: 10; Hosea 10:1). When I called Myself the true vine, I was drawing a parallel between Israel and Myself.

The Greek word *alethine*, meaning "true," is repeatedly used in the Gospel of John to distinguish the reality and My genuineness of Me in contrast to that which is false and unreal. Although in the Old Testament I often talked of Israel as a vine, the image always appears in a negative sense. In contrast, I am the real or genuine vine, a vine that is cared for and carefully pruned by the husbandman and a vine charac-terized by consistent fruit-bearing. Israel was never a vine like this; the nation was a spurious vine that produced sour grapes.

I AM...I AM

The Greek expression *ego eimi*, "I AM," is used in the context of each of My above Jehovistic claims. Simply using the verb *eimi* would have been enough if I had wanted only to draw a parallel between Myself and something else, but the addition of *ego* to this expression draws attention to emphasis. On several occasions I used the expres-sion, "I AM," which includes "Me" as an emphatic subject and verb but failed to supply the predicate (cf. John 4:26; 8:58; 18:5,6,8). This was not a failure on My part to complete a sentence but, rather, an affirmation of My being Jehovah (cf. Exodus 3:14). On at least one occasion My statement was understood by those who heard it in this light, for they responded by picking up stones to kill Me for blasphe-my (John 8:58-59). On another occasion, the uttering of "I AM" was apparently accompanied by a revelation of My glory, which caused the soldiers who had come to arrest Me to fall back under My power (John 18:5-8). I used this expression not just to assert My claims to be *like* Jehovah but to demonstrate that I *was* Jehovah.

CONCLUSION

I am the Jehovah of the Old Testament. All of the names of Jehovah in the Old Testament, therefore, may be applied legitimately to Me (see appendix). I am the eternal contemporary who meets your every need. G. Campbell Morgan once suggested that you could better understand experientially the name Jehovah, I AM, if the verb "to be" were trans-lated "to become." The significance of this name is that Jehovah (Me) is and will become exactly what you need when you feel that need. In this sense, it is an intensely personal and subjective name of Mine. What have I become to you recently?

For Discussion:

1. What is important about the I AMs of the eight Jehovistic titles? How do they reflect My deity?
2. What is the purpose of bread? How do I fulfill this purpose for believers?
3. What did I mean when I described Myself as light?
4. Relate the function of a door to My ministry. What does it mean to go in and out?
5. How am I a good shepherd?
6. What twofold promise is extended because of My title of Resurrection and Life?
7. When I said "I AM . . . I AM," what did I imply? What do you know about Me because of these Jehovistic titles?

CHAPTER ELEVEN

MY CHURCH NAMES

"And I say also unto thee, That thou art Peter, and upon this rock 1 will build my church; and the gates of hell shall not prevail against it" (Matthew 16.18).

Several of My names focus upon My unique relationship to the church. The church is described with many metaphors—such as, the body, a flock of sheep, a bride, a temple or building, and a garden or vineyard. In this connection, I am the Head of the Body, the Shepherd of the Sheep, the Bridegroom of the Bride, the Cornerstone and Master Builder of the Building, and the Vine which gives life to the branches.

I AM THE HEAD OF THE BODY

One of the common images of the church, particularly in the epistles of Paul, is the body of believers. The word "body" is the key word in I Corinthians 12, where the apostle sought to resolve problems at Corinth concerning spiritual gifts. The theme of the Epistle to the Ephesians is the church as My body (Ephesians 5:23). In the Epistle to the Colossians, probably written at the same time as the Ephesian epistle, Paul's theme is to present Me as the Head of the Body (Colossians 1:18).

The "body" is the best known and most used symbol of the church in Scripture. When Paul called Me "the head of the body," he emphasized My authority in and over My church. It was a reminder of My distinctiveness and supremacy. To comprehend this name more fully, you must understand how the apostle used the word "body" to describe the church.

The Greek word *soma*, "body," is used in several ways in the New Testament. On many occasions it refers to the physical body (cf. Romans 1:24; I Corinthians 5:3; Galatians 6:17; I Thessalonians 5:23), but Paul also uses this word to identify the total personality of a man, not just his physical being (cf. Romans 12:1; I Corinthians 13:3, 9:27; Philippians 1:20). It is interesting to note that Paul never uses this word to describe a dead body as is common in Classical Greek and the Septuagint.

Within this context, the church is a living organism, the body of Christ. A local church has a personality and identity which is intimately related to Me its head. The church is a living entity indwelt by Me. Although you must be careful not to make the church more authoritative than the Scriptures (as is common in Catholic traditions), it is important that you recognize the living reality of the church as My body.

If the church is My body, then I Myself am its head (Colossians 1:18; 2:19; Ephesians 1:22-23; 4:15; 5:23). As the head is the determinative center of one's physical being, so I am authoritative in the church. I do not build My church independent of My body but I direct and control the actions of every muscle, organ, and nerve so as to accomplish My will. Part of the mystery of this name is that I, who am omnipotent, should voluntarily choose to limit Myself to working through human beings who, although they are members of My body, retain an independent will by which they can and too often do refuse the directives of the head.

That I am called "the head of the body" implies several truths concerning My relationship to the church. First, it means My purposes cannot be frustrated; I hold ultimate control. Even if one part of the body is rebellious and does not respond to My directives, another will respond. Secondly, it suggests that no individual member within that body can be the organic head of it. Attempts to do so will be frustrated, as in the case of Diotrephes, "who loves to have the preeminence among them" (III John 9). The place of preeminence in the church belongs to Me alone. "And he is the head of the body, the church: who is the beginning, the firstborn from the dead; that in all things he might have the preeminence" (Colossians 1:18).

The practical implication of this title relates to your submission to Me as the head of the body. I demand your obedience to My will and reverential worship of My Person. Anything less falls short of your personal acknowledgment of Me as the Head of the Body.

I AM THE SHEPHERD OF THE SHEEP

Scripture often refers to the church as the flock of God, and so it is not surprising that I should bear the title "Shepherd." When I see the multitudes of people, I see them "scattered abroad, as sheep having no shepherd" (Matthew 9:36). I was the Good Shepherd in My death (John 10:11; Psalm 22), the Great Shepherd in My resurrection (Hebrews 13:20; Psalm 23) and will be the Chief Shepherd in My return to this earth (I Peter 5:4; Psalm 24). Unlike the hireling whose primary concern is himself, I care for My sheep. I have entrusted the care of parts of My flock to others called "pastors," or more literally, "shepherds." As the shepherd I am the model for pastors in caring for the flock. The title "shepherd" was also one of My Jehovistic names in the Gospel of John.

I AM THE BRIDEGROOM OF THE BRIDE

When John the Baptist became the first to call Me "the bridegroom" (John 3:29), the term was already rich in meaning. The Old Testament frequently portrayed Israel as the wife of the Lord (Isaiah 54:6; Jeremiah 31:32; Hosea 2:1-23). As John the Baptist on that occasion noted, "He that hath the bride is the bridegroom" (John 3:29). This title was to have special significance in the New Testament, not for Israel as the wife of God but, rather, for the church, which is My bride. The relation between the bride and Bridegroom is most fully taught in a passage in which the Apostle Paul addresses several principles of family living (Ephesians 5:25-27). These verses emphasize that I loved the church, gave Myself for it, purposes to sanctify and cleanse it by the Word of God, and promises to take it to Myself as a perfected bride. My work began in eternity past when I determined to die for her because of My love for her and will be consummated in the new Jerusalem when you shall with John see "the holy city, new Jerusalem, coming down from God out of heaven, prepared as a bride adorned for her husband" (Revelation 21:2).

The image of the bride and Bridegroom serves to emphasize the need for qualitative or spiritual church growth—that is, growth in your love for Me. The church was "espoused" to Me by the apostles (II Corinthians 11:2) and should grow closer to Me during the "engagement period" of this present age. Unfortunately, the history of the professing church suggests she has been as unfaithful to her Groom as Israel was to her Husband.

I AM THE CORNERSTONE AND FOUNDATION OF THE BUILDING

I am called "a stone" or "rock" in three different meanings in the Scripture. To Israel I am a "stumbling" stone or "a rock of offence" (Isaiah 8:14,15; Romans 9:32,33; I Corinthians 1:23; I Peter 2:8). To the world I am the smiting stone, which will destroy the antichrist kingdoms of the world (Daniel 2:34). But to the church, I am the cornerstone of the church, which I am presently building. "The stone which the builders disallowed, the same is made the head of the corner" (I Peter 2:7).

Some of the significance of this title has been lost to the average Christian today because of changes in architectural design in the centuries. The Greek word *lithos*, "stone," was used of ordinary field stones that were found on the ground. It was common in the construction of first-century buildings to lean the building on itself. This meant that one part of the structure would have a greater amount of pressure on it than the rest of the structure. Over the years, the materials used in this area would wear faster. To compensate for this, builders sought for a hard field stone upon which the structure would rest. It became known as the cornerstone and was the one part of the building on which the rest of the structure depended absolutely.

When the apostles called Me "the Cornerstone," they were not thinking of the decorative marble slab affixed to a building after construction was finished. Rather, a cornerstone is the foundational rock upon which the building would depend for its stability and strength. In the "temple of God," the church, I am the "head of the corner," which gives both strength and stability to the spiritual temple of believers who are also likened to the stones with which the rest of building is constructed (1 Peter 2:5).

I AM THE TRUE VINE AND THE BRANCHES

In the Old Testament, God often used the image of a vine or vine-yard to describe the nation Israel (Psalm 80:8; Isaiah 5:1-7; Jeremiah 2:21; Ezekiel 15; 19:10; Hosea 10:1), but always the image was that of an unkempt vineyard which had gone wild. I called Myself, in contrast, the true vine and identified My disciples as the branches of that vine (John 15:1-8). This is perhaps the most intimate of images used in Scripture to describe the oneness of Me and believers. I am not the stem from which the branches grow but the vine, which is the total life of the branches. The image of a vine is better suited than that of a tree, for the vine and branches grow into one another so that it is difficult to distinguish the vine from the branches. That ought also to be true of the relationship of the believer to Me.

This title, "the Vine," is the seventh of My Jehovistic titles in the Gospel of John, and further aspects of this title are discussed elsewhere in this book. The practical application of this title to the church relates to its oneness with Me. The church's responsibility is to grow spiritually, and to bear fruit consistently, but it needs occasional pruning from Me.

Because I am the vine and you are the branches, you can accomplish nothing apart from Me. I am the supplier and sustainer of the very life of the believer, and the Christian life is lived by faith in Me (cf. Galatians 2:20). As I live My life through you, you will bear fruit. This fruit will consist of both converts to Me, and your development of godly character, which the Apostle Paul describes as the fruit of the Holy Spirit (Galatians 5:22-23). Your primary responsibility is to abide in Me.

From time to time in your Christian lives, you encounter difficult and trying circumstances. Many times they are of the sort which allow you to seek spiritual causes. Many Christians mistakenly conclude that problems in the Christian life are always caused by sin. They are convinced they have committed some sin which they are ignorant of. What they fail to realize, however, is that some troubles in the Christian life are the result of their faithfulness. One of My forgotten promises is that I will reward fruitfulness with pruning, so you "may bring forth more fruit" (John 15:2). By using a different metaphor, Job expressed this same hope in the midst of his trial: "But he knows the way that I take: when he hath tried me, I shall come forth as gold" (Job 23:10).

CONCLUSION

My titles mentioned above are significant, for they reveal who I am in relation to My people. This emphasis is so common in Scripture as to be taken for granted. In most religious systems, the deity of that religion is to be feared, served, and sacrificed to. But I delight not in keeping My distance from My people. But I delight in developing a greater intimacy with them.

Although I do relate individually to My disciples, it is interesting that many of My names should relate to the church. During the sixties, the mood of America was largely anti-institutional, and many Christians were infected with a spirit of rejecting the church. Things have changed to some degree since then, but many Christians are still somewhat anti-church. Remember that I love the church and gave Myself for her and have great plans for her in the days to come. Christians who voluntarily divorce themselves from the church and fail to belong to, support, and pray for their local, Bible-believing church are placing themselves in a position in which they can hardly experience the rich reality of My church names.

For Discussion:

1. Discuss My five titles mentioned in this chapter. What unique ministry is highlighted in each title?
2. How may you express your submission to Me as the Head of the Body?
3. Discuss how I the Shepherd am the model for pastors in caring for the flock.
4. As a Bridegroom, what do I do for those who are My bride?
5. List several contributions that a foundation makes to a building. How do these relate to the believer's life and to Me, their cornerstone?
6. Why do I add the qualifying term "true" when I call Myself a vine? How do I the vine relate to believers as branches?

CHAPTER TWELVE

MY APOCALYPTIC NAMES

"The Revelation of Jesus Christ, which God gave unto him, to shew unto his servants things which must shortly come to pass; and he sent and signified it by his angel unto his servant John"
(Revelation 1:1).

The final book of the New Testament offers the fullest revelation of Me in Scripture. Even its divinely inspired title states its purpose as "The Revelation of Jesus Christ" (Revelation 1:1). It is not, therefore, surprising that this book contains over seventy of My names and titles. In reading the Revelation, many people get sidetracked by focusing on obscure symbols or strained interpretations of things to come. But ultimately, when you look at this book, you ought to see Me. Note carefully My seventy-two names and titles in this book. I am called . . .

Jesus Christ (1:1), word of God (1:2), the Faithful Witness, the first begotten of the dead, and the prince of the kings of the earth (1:5), the Alpha and Omega, the beginning and the ending, the Lord, and the Almighty (1:8), the first and the last (1:11), the voice (1:12), the Son of man (1:13), he that liveth (1:18), he that holds the seven stars and he who walks in the midst of the seven golden candlesticks (2:1), he who was dead and is alive (2:8), he who hath the sharp sword with two edges (2:12), the hidden manna (2:17), the Son of God (2:18), the morning star (2:28), he that hath the seven Spirits of God and he that hath the seven stars (3:1), he that is holy, he that is true, he that hath the key of David, he that opens and he that shuts (3:7), my new name (3:12), the Amen, the faithful and true witness, and the beginning of the creation of God (3:14), Lord God Almighty (4:8), worthy (4:11), the Lion of the tribe of Judah and the Root of David (5:5), a Lamb (5:6), the Lamb that was slain (5:12), Lord holy and true (6:10), him that sitteth on the throne (6:16), the Lamb who is in the midst of the throne (7:17), him that liveth forever and ever and he who created (10:6), our Lord (11:8), his Christ (11:15), her child (12:4), a man child (12:5), the Lamb slain from the foundation of the world (13:8), Jesus (14:12), King of saints (15:3), who art, and wast, and shalt be (16:5), who hath power over these plagues (16:9), God Almighty (16:14), Lord of lords and King of kings (17:14), the Lord God who judges her (18:8), the Lord our God (19:1), God that sat on the throne (19:4), Lord God omnipotent (19:6), Faithful and True (19:11), a name written that no man knew (19:12), the Word of God (19:13), Christ (20:4), husband (21:2), God (21:7), the glory of God (21:23), the Lord God of the holy prophets (22:6), the root and offspring of David and the bright and morning star (22:16), he who testifies these things and Lord Jesus (22:20), our Lord Jesus Christ (22:21).

John was a climactic writer. Like all good writers, he developed his own style. When he wrote, he did so under inspiration and expressed himself climactically. In his Gospel, he builds his case until the reader comes to the climax of the book and falls on his face to declare with Thomas that Jesus is, "My Lord and my God" (John 20:28). Climactically, he wrote the last of the four Gospels. Climactically, he was the last person to write Scripture. Climactically, his Gospel is the greatest thesis on Me. Climactically, his book was the last to be recognized as canonical. Climactically, he wrote the last book of the Bible. Climactically, he wrote concerning the last things. In baseball, you have to have a finisher, that is, the relief pitcher. If anyone was God's relief pitcher, it was the Apostle John. It should almost be expected that John would be the one chosen of God to give such a full and rich description of Me in My names.

This profusion of names and titles, many highly symbolic in meaning in keeping with the nature of the book, provides a composite portrait of My person. It is truly a "revelation of Jesus Christ" in My names. It is perhaps the fullest description in the New Testament of the majesty of My Being.

Obviously, within the space limitations of this chapter you cannot study all of My seventy-two names in the final book of the Bible. What you will do, however, is examine several groups or principal names. An examination of these names makes you increasingly aware that I can meet any and every need you might have.

I AM JESUS CHRIST

In his brief introduction to the book, John first uses the name "Jesus Christ" (1:1). This is a composite of My personal and official names. By the end of the first century, this had become a common way to refer to Me. In a sense, it represented a synthesization of the New Testament. My name Jesus is the predominant name in the Gospels and Acts, whereas Christ is the predominant name in the Epistles, especially the Pauline epistles. You examined both of these names closely in earlier chapters.

A Threefold Picture of Me

John goes on to describe Me, "Jesus Christ, who is the faithful witness, and the first begotten of the dead, and the prince of the kings of the earth" (1:5). This introduces in this book the three primary ideas concerning who I am. It is typical throughout the writings of John that although he writes in Greek, his thinking is controlled by his Hebrew heritage. It is not, therefore, surprising that the Revelation should focus on the threefold Messianic office of prophet, priest, and king.

I am first, the prophet; John identifies Me as "the faithful witness." I came to reveal the Father to mankind and did so perfectly (cf. Matthew 11:27). The Greek word translated "witness" here is *martus*, from which you get the English term "martyr." Originally, *martus* meant "a witness" but came to refer to one who died because of his faithfulness in witnessing. It is interesting to note that I Myself later applied this title to a believer in Pergamum named Antipas (Revelation 2:13). The implication is that just as I am the faithful witness of the Father to you, you need to be faithful witnesses of Me to the world. This title must have been very meaningful to John, who was himself exiled on Patmos because of his faithful witness of the things of God.

The second of these three titles in Revelation 1:5 emphasizes My role as a priest; I am "the first begotten of the dead." In the Epistle to the Hebrews, I who arose became the high priest. I was the first to rise to eternal life. Others had been raised before but later died again.

Theologians call these "resuscitations" as opposed to "resurrections." Also unique concerning My resurrection is the fact that I was raised not only to live forever but also to become "a quickening [or life-giving] spirit" (I Corinthians 15:45; Colossians 1:18).

Thirdly, Revelation 1:5 calls Me "the prince of the kings of the earth." Although not denying My sovereignty now as the authority by which kings rule (Romans 13: 1) and the "Lord of all" (Acts 10:36), this book emphasizes My coming dominion upon this earth. In this sense, it is right for John to refer to Me not only as "king" but also as "prince." A man is a prince until he formally assumes office as king. The next monarch of the British Commonwealth is called Prince. Even though he is trained to be king and will someday assume the throne until the Queen dies or surrenders the throne, the prince will remain a prince. At the beginning of the book of Revelation, I am called a prince of kings, but when I come to establish My kingdom on earth, I am called "KING OF KINGS, AND LORD OF LORDS" (19:16).

MY ETERNAL COMPLETENESS AND SUFFICIENCY

Another significant grouping of names appears in Revelation 1:8. The first of these four titles is the "Alpha and Omega." This is the Greek expression of a Hebrew idiom that implies completeness. The Jews took the first and last letters of their alphabet to emphasize and express the entirety of a thing. Alpha is the first letter of the Greek alphabet; omega is the last. A similar English expression is "everything from A to Z." In a sense, this title includes all of My more than 700 names and titles (see Appendix where My names and titles are listed alphabetically).

In the second of this grouping of names, I am identified as "the beginning and the ending." I am the One who not only pioneers or initiates but also perfects or finishes (cf. Hebrews 12:2). This title serves to emphasize My absolute sovereignty over history. I am the Lord of history, its beginning, its ending, and all that lies between. Although I may not yet be sitting on the throne of David in Jerusalem, nevertheless, I have control and a unique way of working through others, even using tyrants and terrorists at times to accomplish My purpose (cf. Romans 8:28).

Thirdly, Revelation 1:8 describes Me as "the Lord, which is, and which was, and which is to come." There could be no more specific statement of My deity and eternality. This title parallels Moses' great affirmation of faith, "From everlasting to everlasting, thou art God" (Psalm 90:2). I am eternally contemporary, the "I am" of all times. The writer of the Hebrews speaks of Me: "Jesus Christ the same yesterday, and today, and forever" (Hebrews 13:8).

Finally, I am called "the Almighty." This title probably was not intended to emphasize My omnipotence, although that attribute of God is certainly implied. Possibly John was thinking in the context of *El Shaddai*, an Old Testament title of God usually translated "God Almighty." Are you trusting Me with your problems in life?

I AM THE SON OF MAN

More than any other book in the New Testament, the book of Revelation draws from the Old Testament, particularly from the Messianic prophecies of the Old Testament. Much of the first three chapters of the Revelation describes Me as a vision giving My message to seven churches. In this context, John uses many names and titles, but now John introduces Me as "one like unto the Son of man" (1:13). Most conservative commentators agree that this is a reference to Me, the One Daniel called "the Son of man" (Daniel 7:13), who received "dominion, and glory, and a kingdom" from the Ancient of Days (verse 14).

When John turned to see the voice that spoke to him, the first things he observed were seven golden candlesticks. These candlesticks were probably not the kind which decorate homes but, rather, the candlesticks used in Jewish worship. They stood about five feet, five inches tall and weighed about one hundred ten pounds each. They branched out on top to hold several candles; thus, many lights produced the one light of the candlestick. I explain that these candlesticks represent seven local churches in Asia (1:20). It is interesting to note that I was "in the middle of the seven candlesticks"—that is, an equal distance from each of them. I was as close to the church in delinquency as I was to the church in revival. Why? Because the whole church is My body.

John pictured Me here in the garment of the priest. This vivid description of Me as I stood glorified and transfigured before the apostle, tends to emphasize My role as a judge. My head and hair were "white like wool, as white as snow" (1:14), a symbol of My purity. "His eyes were as a flame of fire" (1:14)—that is, they burned through the one whom they saw to discern accurately the nature of man. My feet were compared to "fine brass, as if they burned in a furnace" (1:15). Throughout the Scripture, brass, or more correctly bronze, is offered as a symbol of judgment. My voice is here compared to "the sound of many waters" (1:15), emphasizing My authority. "Out of his mouth went a sharp two-edged sword" (1:16), a symbol of the Word of God in its discerning power (cf. Hebrews 4:12). There was a brilliance about My entire countenance "as the sun shineth in his strength" (1:16).

There in My presence—glorified, transfigured,—John fell prostrate to the ground. Like the Old Testament prophets, John was learning experientially that if you really want to do something for God, you begin in My presence. Greatness always begins in My presence, not at a seminary or Bible college.

This vision of Me was significant in every detail—from My seven epistles to the seven churches in chapters two and three. Each name I used to identify Myself represented My ability to meet the particular need of each church. As you have studied My names, I trust you have already discovered that whatever your need today, I can meet that need.

The first of the seven churches which I addressed was the church at Ephesus. This was a commendable church in many respects, but it had begun to wander from its first love. The church needed leadership which would boldly direct the church back to the place from which they had fallen. To that church, I identified Myself as "He that holdeth the seven stars in his right hand" (2:1). Earlier John had been told that the stars were the angels or messengers—that is, the pastors of the churches (Revelation 1:20). The senior pastor of the church at Ephesus needed to be encouraged that he was in My right hand as he undertook to lead the flock in that city.

The church at Smyrna was a congregation under intense persecution. Many of their members had already lost their lives because of their faithfulness, and many more would do so in the days to come. They are not criticized in any way by Me, only encouraged to remain faithful. To encourage this church, I reminded them I was "the first and the last, which was dead, and is alive" (2:8).

Unlike the above churches, the church at Pergamum (or Pergamos) was a congregation with a mixed multitude. Some of its members gave no evidence of being saved. They were somewhat lax in their standards of personal separation and engaged in activities most of the Christians of that day considered wrong. It was a church that was bending to social pressure to conform to the standard of the world. As a result it had begun wandering away from their commitment to biblical authority. More than anything else, the church needed a "back-to-the-Bible revival." To this church, I revealed Myself as "he who hath the sharp sword with two edges" (2:12)—that is, the Word of God.

The church at Thyatira was one which would probably have been rejected as a legitimate church by most evangelical definitions today. A prominent woman in the church was introducing several pagan practices into the church, including immorality and idolatry. Of these two named sins, I appear to be most concerned with her refusal to repent of fornication. As a result, I introduced Myself to that church as the Son of God coming in judgment with My burning eyes and bronze feet (2:18).

The next church I addressed was the church at Sardis. It was a very reputable church, but in many respects its reputation was all it had. Some commentators identify this church with the Reformation movement in the sixteenth and seventeenth century. The church is described as dead but still possessing a believing remnant. Although the Reformers helped the church greatly with their reemphasis upon the doctrines of grace, they failed to be as effective as they could be because they neglected the evangelistic work of the Holy Spirit. Significantly, I reminded this church that I was "he that hath the seven Spirits of God" who addressed them (3:1).

In many respects, the church at Philadelphia enjoyed the most coveted of circumstances among the seven churches. Again, there is nothing I chose to criticize directly. Although the church was small, it had unprecedented opportunities for service ahead of it. It was a church in the midst of revival and simply needed to be reminded not to allow the revival to degenerate into an emotional fanaticism. To this church I identified Myself as "he that is holy, he that is true, he that hath the key of David" (3:7). The reference to "the key of David" originates in Isaiah 22:22 and emphasizes that I alone have authority to admit whom I wish into the kingdom. This church needed truth and holiness, but it also needed to grasp the opportunities that awaited them in reaching their world with the gospel.

The church of Laodicea has come to represent the lukewarm compromise often characteristic of many churches today. They needed to be reminded who I was as "the Amen, the faithful and true witness, the beginning of the creation of God" (3:14). To this church I was the final word, an example that one could be both faithful and true. It was also a reminder that as Creator, I knew what was best for My church in Laodicea.

I AM THE LION AND THE LAMB

One of the most interesting contrasts of names in Revelation occurs in chapter five, where in the same context I am called both "the Lion of the tribe of Judah" and "a Lamb" (5:5-6). If this combination sounds paradoxical in English, it is even more so in Greek. The word used here for "lamb" is a diminutive and a term of endearment. It is the sort of word a child might use to describe a cute and cuddly baby lamb. And yet, this title is used here in the context of the regal majesty of the Lion of the tribe of Judah, the ruling tribe of Israel.

John here brings together two titles with different emphases to give his readers a fuller understanding of who I am. As the Lion, I am everything the Jews expected in their Messiah. I was the son of David who would rule over Caesar. I was the One coming to establish the kingdom of God on earth. But I was also the Messiah who came to give My life a ransom for many. As such, I am the sacrificial yearling lamb. But I am a lamb with a difference: this lamb had seven horns. A horn was a symbol of power in the Old Testament, and seven was a number of completeness in Scripture. This is the lamb with the fullness of the strength and power of the lion.

When Samson sought to give the Philistines a riddle they could not resolve on their own, he said, "Out of the strong came forth sweetness" (Judges 14:14). Even today, it is uncommon to find strength and sweetness in the same thing. But I manifested both strength and beauty. As you survey My many names and titles, you note some which emphasize My strength at the same time that others tend to emphasize My gentleness. This is evident in Revelation which emphasizes the fact that God still sits on the throne and will ultimately triumph over the world system: yet, twenty-six times you learn that I am the Lamb. My predominant name in Revelation is "the Lamb."

I AM THE COMING CONQUEROR

The plot of the book of Revelation, particularly from chapter four to the end, views Me as the legitimate One to possess the title-deed of the world. Revelation examines the preparations in heaven and events on earth which are necessary for Me to claim what is rightfully Mine and to establish My kingdom. This plot reaches a climax in chapter nineteen, where My second coming in glory is described. In that passage, I am identified by five significant names (19:11-16).

The first of My conquering names is "Faithful and True" (19:11). Faith/faithfulness and truth are constant themes in the writings of John. I had been identified by these names earlier in Revelation, but for emphasis, the compound name appears here at the climax. Right to the end, I am faithful. Right to the end, I am true. This is a tremendous encouragement in times of trials; even the finest of Christians begin to wonder, "Is it really worth all this?" Regardless of your circumstances, regardless of your situation, and regardless of how long your circumstances have been like this, I will prove Myself to be faithful and true right to the end.

The second name John records in this passage is "a name written, that no man knew, but he himself" (19:12). This may be one of the most fascinating of all My names. Several years ago Elmer Towns became interested in discovering My names in Scripture. Originally, he compiled a listing of about 250 names and thought he had exhausted the topic. Yet, as he continued to read and study the Scripture, he came across names that were not on My list. He had heard someone once say that there were 365 names for Me, one for each day of the year, and wondered whether that was so. To date, he has found over 700 names, and he is no longer convinced that even this longer list is exhaustive. Each time he discovers a new name, he is impressed again by another attribute or aspect of My work which a name suggests.

As much as he wants to know all My names, he realizes that even at My return there will be an element of mystery about at least one of My names. When you consider all that is involved in each of the names listed in the appendix of this book, it is clear there is no limit to all I am in regard to My names. It would be futile for you even to try to speculate as to the particular significance of this unknown name in Revelation 19:12. Its presence in Scripture reminds you again I have a name for every need, even if you don't know the name specifically.

Thirdly, I am called "The Word of God" (19:13). I am the idea or expression of God Himself. This is also one of My birth names, "*Logos*" that was dealt with in the chapter of My birth names. A fourth name mentioned in this passage is "Almighty God" (19:15), which may refer to *El Shaddai* or, in this context, the divine omnipotence which is another one of My attributes.

Finally, John notes the published name embroidered into My garment, "KING OF KINGS, AND LORD OF LORDS" (19:16). With this title I come, followed by the armies of heaven, which may be an angelic host or more probably the raptured saints. Although you may not be much of a rider on horseback today, someday you may ride in that heavenly cavalry behind Me, the King of kings and Lord of lords. This title emphasizes My absolute sovereignty.

I AM THE ROOT AND OFFSPRING OF DAVID

In the closing verses of this book, I identify Myself as "the root and offspring of David" (22:16). This name suggests two ideas in My relationship with David. The first is that of an old root buried in the ground, which from time to time sends up shoots or "suckers" as they are sometimes called. The sucker draws all its strength and nourishment from the root. Those in charge of orchards are continually watching for these new shoots and pruning them back so that the original fruit tree is not robbed of any nourishment the root might otherwise supply to it. I was David's source of strength and nourishment, just as a root supplies the shoot with its strength and nourishment. What was true in David's experience with Me is also true in the experience of believers today: You derive everything you need from Me.

But I was not only the source of David but also the seed of David. As the offspring of David, I was the legitimate heir to the throne of David. I was the qualified candidate in which all the Messianic prophecies concerning David's greater Son were or shall be fulfilled. I was the Son of David and also David's Lord (Mark 12:35-37). This title was rich in Jewish heritage, for David was considered the model king of Israel.

I AM THE BRIGHT AND MORNING STAR

Again, in identifying another of My titles, the Scriptures refer to an image of light. I call Myself "the bright and morning star" (22:16). This star is so named because it appears on the horizon just before sunrise. The appearance of the morning star tells you that the "dayspring from on high" is almost here. It is the star of hope for those who are tired of the long night of darkness. And with the Apostle John, you are encouraged by this star to pray, "Even so, come, Lord Jesus" (22:20).

CONCLUSION

If I were to come to you today and ask, "What could I do for you?" how would you respond? Actually, the question is not hypothetical. I am here and asking. I want to become more meaningful in your life by revealing Myself in My names to you. I trust you have learned something new about Me in this brief study of My names, but I hope even more that your new knowledge of Me goes beyond your intellect. My names and titles in Scripture become ever clearer in the context of your experience with Me. Don't be the barrier that prevents Me from doing for you what I want to do in order to make My names a meaningful part of your Christian experience.

For Discussion:

1. Why does the last book in the Bible, Revelation, have perhaps more of My names than any other? What is the main theme of this book?
2. Why is Revelation called a climactic book?
3. What is the threefold picture of Me in Revelation? Relate it to My threefold anointed offices.
4. Note the contrasting descriptions of Me as a Lion and Lamb. How do these titles carry out the theme of Revelation? What do these titles tell you about Me?
5. Name the titles in Revelation that describe Me as a conqueror. What do these titles tell you about Me?
6. Explain how I am the Root and Offspring of David.
7. Share briefly something new you have learned about Me in this study of My names.

MY NAMES AND TITLES
IN SCRIPTURE

A-21

The Advocate with the Father ....(I John 2:1)
Aijeleth Shahar .... (Psalm 22:Title)
An Alien unto My Mother's Children .... (Psalm 69:8)
Alive for Evermore .... (Revelation 1:18)
The All, and in All .... (Colossians 3:11)
The Almighty Which Is .... (Revelation 1:8)
The Alpha and Omega .... (Revelation 1:8)
An Altar .... (Hebrews 13:10)
The Altogether Lovely .... (Song of Solomon 5:16)
The Amen .... (Revelation 3:14)
The Angel of the Covenant..(Malachi 3:1)
The Angel of God .... (Genesis 21:17)
The Angel of His Presence .... (Isaiah 63:9)
The Angel of the Lord .... (Genesis 16:7)
The Anointed of God ....(I Samuel 2:35; Psalm 2:2)
Another King .... (Acts 17:7)
The Apostle of Our Profession ....(Hebrews 3:1)
The Ark of the Covenant .... (Joshua 3:3)
The Arm of the Lord .... (Isaiah 53:1)
The Author of Eternal Salvation .... (Hebrews 5:9)
The Author of Our Faith ....(Hebrews 12:2)

B – 32

The Babe of Bethlehem ....(Luke 2:12, 16)
The Balm in Gilead .... (Jeremiah 8:22)
A Banner to Them that Fear Thee .... (Psalm 60:4)
The Bearer of Glory ....(Zechariah 6:13)
The Bearer of Sin .... (Hebrews 9:28)

The Beauties of Holiness .... (Psalm 110:3)
Before All Things .... (Colossians 1:17)
The Beginning .... (Colossians 1:18)
The Beginning of the Creation of God .... (Revelation 3:14)
The Beginning and the Ending .... (Revelation 1:8)
The Beloved .... (Ephesians 1:6)
My Beloved Son .... (Matthew 3:17)
The Better .... (Hebrews 7:7)
The Bishop of Your Souls .... (I Peter 2:25)
The Blessed and Only Potentate .... (I Timothy 6:15)
The Blessed for Evermore .... (II Corinthians 11:31)
The Blessed Hope .... (Titus 2:13)
The Branch .... (Zechariah 3:8; 6:12)
The Branch of the Lord .... (Isaiah 4:2)
The Branch of Righteousness .... (Jeremiah 33:15)
The Branch Out of His Roots .... (Isaiah 11:1)
The Bread of God .... (John 6:33)
The Bread of Life .... (John 6:35)
The Breaker .... (Micah 2:13)
The Bridegroom of the Bride .... (John 3:29)
The Bright and Morning Star .... (Revelation 22:16)
The Brightness of His Glory .... (Hebrews 1:3)
The Brightness of Thy Rising .... (Isaiah 60:3)
Our Brother .... (Matthew 12:50)
A Buckler .... (Psalm 18:30)
The Builder of the Temple .... (Zechariah 6:12-13)
A Bundle of Myrrh .... (Song of Solomon 1:13)

C -40

The Captain of the Hosts of the Lord .... (Joshua 5:14-15)
The Captain of Their Salvation .... (Hebrews 2:10)
The Carpenter .... (Mark 6:3)
The Carpenter's Son .... (Matthew 13:55)
A Certain Nobleman .... (Luke 19:12)
A Certain Samaritan .... (Luke 10:33)
The Chief Cornerstone .... (Ephesians 2:20; I Peter 2:6)
The Chief Shepherd .... (I Peter 5:4)

The Chiefest Among Ten Thousand .... (Song of Solomon 5:10)
A Child Born .... (Isaiah 9:6)
Child of the Holy Ghost .... (Matthew 1:18)
The Child Jesus ....(Luke 2:27, 43)
The Chosen of God .... (I Peter 2:4)
Chosen out of the People .... (Psalm 89:19)
Christ .... (Matthew 1:16)
The Christ ....(I John 5: 1)
Christ Come in the Flesh ....(I John 4:2)
Christ Crucified .... (I Corinthians 1:23)
The Christ of God ....(Luke 9:20)
Christ Jesus ....(Acts 19:4)
Christ Jesus the Lord .... (II Corinthians 4:5)
Christ a King ....(Luke 23:2)
Christ the Lord ....(Luke 2: 11)
Christ Our Passover .... (I Corinthians 5:7)
Christ Risen from the Dead .... (I Corinthians 15:20)
The Chosen of God ....(Luke 23:35)
A Cleft of the Rock .... (Exodus 33:22)
A Cluster of Camphire .... (Song of Solomon 1:14)
The Comforter ....(John 14:16-18)
A Commander to the Peoples .... (Isaiah 55:4)
Conceived of the Holy Spirit .... (Matthew 1:20)
The Consolation of Israel ....(Luke 2:25)
The Corn of Wheat ....(John 12:24)
Counselor .... (Isaiah 9:6)
The Covenant of the People .... (Isaiah 42:6; 49:8)
The Covert from the Tempest .... (Isaiah 32:2)
The Covert of Thy Wings .... (Psalm 61:4)
The Creator ....(Romans 1:25)
The Creator of the Ends of the Earth .... (Isaiah 40:28)
A Crown of Glory .... (Isaiah 28:5)

D-17

My Darling .... (Psalm 22:20)
David .... (Matthew 1:17)
The Day ....(II Peter 1:19)

The Daysman Betwixt Us .... (Job 9:33)
The Dayspring from on High ....(Luke 1:78)
The Daystar to Arise .... (II Peter 1:19)
His Dear Son .... (Colossians 1:13)
That Deceiver .... (Matthew 27:63)
My Defense .... (Psalm 94:22)
The Deliverance of Zion .... (Joel 2:32)
My Deliverer .... (Psalm 40:17)
The Desire of All Nations .... (Haggai 2:7)
Despised by the People .... (Psalm 22:6)
The Dew of Israel .... (Hosea 14:5)
A Diadem of Beauty .... (Isaiah 28:5)
The Door of the Sheep ....(John 10:7)
Dwelling Place .... (Psalm 90:1)

E-17

Mine Elect .... (Isaiah 42:1)
Eliakim .... (Isaiah 22:20)
Elijah .... (Matthew 16:14)
Emmanuel .... (Matthew 1:23)
The End of the Law...(Romans 10:4)
The Ensign of the People .... (Isaiah 11:10)
Equal with God .... (Philippians 2:6)
The Eternal God ....(Deuteronomy 33:27)
That Eternal Life ....(I John 1:2)
The Everlasting Father... (Isaiah 9:6)
An Everlasting Light.. (Isaiah 60:19,20)
An Everlasting Name .... (Isaiah 63:12)
Thy Exceedingly Great Reward .... (Genesis 15:1)
His Excellency .... (Job 13:11)
The Excellency of Our God .... (Isaiah 35:2)
Excellent .... (Psalm 8:1,9)
The Express Image of His Person ....(Hebrews 1:3)

F – 38

The Face of the Lord ....(Luke 1:76)
The Fairer than the Children of Men .... (Psalm 45:2)

Faithful .... (I Thessalonians 5:24)
Faithful and True .... (Revelation 19:11)
The Faithful and True Witness .... (Revelation 3:14)
A Faithful Creator .... (I Peter 4:19)
A Faithful High Priest .... (Hebrews 2:17)
A Faithful Priest .... (I Samuel 2:35)
The Faithful Witness .... (Revelation 1:5)
A Faithful Witness Between Us .... (Jeremiah 42:5)
A Faithful Witness in Heaven .... (Psalm 89:37)
My Father .... (Psalm 89:26)
A Father of the Fatherless .... (Psalm 68:5)
The Feast .... (I Corinthians 5:8)
My Fellow .... (Zechariah 13:7)
The Finisher of the Faith .... (Hebrews 12:2)
The First and the Last .... (Revelation 1:8)
The First Begotten .... (Hebrews 1:6)
The Firstborn .... (Hebrews 12:23)
The Firstborn among Many Brethren .... (Romans 8:29)
The Firstborn of the Dead ....(Revelation 1:5-KJV "begotten")
The Firstborn of Every Creature .... (Colossians 1:15)
Her Firstborn Son .... (Luke 2:7)
The First Fruit .... (Romans 11:16)
The Firstfruits of Them That Sleep .... (I Corinthians 15:20)
Flesh .... (John 1:14)
The Foolishness of God .... (I Corinthians 1:25)
Foreordained before the Foundation of the World .... (I Peter 1:20)
The Forerunner .... (Hebrews 6:20)
Fortress .... (Psalm 18:2).
The Foundation Which Is Laid .... (I Corinthians 3:11)
The Fountain of Life .... (Psalm 36:9)
The Fountain of Living Waters ....(Jeremiah 17:13)
The Free Gift ....(Romans 5:15)
The Friend of Publicans and Sinners ....(Matthew 11:9; Luke 7:34)
A Friend that Sticketh Closer than a Brother .... (Proverbs 18:24)
The Fruit of the Earth .... (Isaiah 4:2)
The Fruit of Thy Womb ....(Luke 1:42)
Fullers' Soap ....(Malachi 3:2)

G – 47

The Gift of God	(John 4:10)
A Gin	(Isaiah 8:14)
A Glorious High Throne from the Beginning	(Jeremiah 17:12)
A Glorious Name	(Isaiah 63:14)
Glory	(Haggai 2:7)
My Glory	(Psalm 3:3)
The Glory as of the Only Begotten of the Father	(John 1:14)
The Glory of God	(Romans 3:23)
The Glory of His Father	(Matthew 16:27; Mark 8:38)
God	(Revelation 21:7)
God Who Avengeth Me	(Psalm 18:47)
God Blessed Forever	(Romans 9:5)
God Who Forgavest Them	(Psalm 99:8)
Our God Forever and Ever	(Psalm 48:14)
The God of Glory	(Psalm 29:3)
The God of Israel	(Psalm 59:5)
The God of Jacob	(Psalm 46:7)
The God of My Life	(Psalm 42:8)
The God of My Mercy	(Psalm 59:10)
God in the Midst of Her	(Psalm 46:5)
God Manifest in the Flesh	(I Timothy 3:16)
God of My Righteousness	(Psalm 4:1)
God of My Salvation	(Psalm 18:46; 24:5)
God of My Strength	(Psalm 43:2)
God with Us	(Matthew 1:23)
A Good Man	(John 7:12)
The Goodman of the House	(Matthew 20:11)
Good Master	(Matthew 19:16)
The Good Shepherd	(John 10:11)
The Governor Among Nations	(Psalm 22:28)
Great	(Jeremiah 32:18)
The Great God	(Titus 2:13)
A Great High Priest	(Hebrews 4:14)
A Great Light	(Isaiah 9:2)
A Great Prophet	(Luke 7:16)
That Great Shepherd of the Sheep	(Hebrews 13:20)

Greater ....(I John 4:4)
A Greater and More Perfect Tabernacle ....(Hebrews 9:11)
Greater Than Our Father Abraham ....(John 8:53, 57-58)
Greater Than Our Father Jacob ....(John 4:12)
Greater Than Jonah .... (Matthew 12:41)
Greater Than Solomon.. (Matthew 12:42)
Greater Than the Temple .... (Matthew 12:6)
Guest ....(Luke 19:7)
Our Guide Even Unto Death .... (Psalm 48:14)
The Guide of My Youth ....(Jeremiah 3:4)
The Guiltless .... (Matthew 12:7)

H -41

The Habitation of Justice ....(Jeremiah 50:7)
Harmless ....(Hebrews 7:26)
An He Goat .... (Proverbs 30:31)
The Head of All Principality and Power .... (Colossians 2:10)
The Head of Every Man .... (I Corinthians 11:3)
The Head of the Body, the Church .... (Colossians 1:18)
The Head of the Corner .... (I Peter 2:7)
The Health of My Countenance .... (Psalm 42:11)
The Heir ....(Mark 12:7)
Heir of All Things ....(Hebrews 1:2)
My Helper ....(Hebrews 13:6; Psalm 32:7)
The Helper of the Fatherless .... (Psalm 10:14)
A Hen .... (Matthew 23:37)
The Hidden Manna .... (Revelation 2:17)
My Hiding Place .... (Psalm 32:7)
A Hiding Place from the Wind .... (Isaiah 32:2)
The High and Lofty One Who Inhabiteth Eternity ..... (Isaiah 57:15)
An High Priest ....(Hebrews 5:5)
An High Priest after the Order of Melchisedek ....(Hebrews 5:10)
An High Priest Forever ....(Hebrews 6:20)
My High Tower .... (Psalm 18:2)
The Highest Himself .... (Psalm 87:5)
An Highway .... (Isaiah 35:8)
Holy .... (Isaiah 57:15)

Thy Holy Child Jesus ....(Acts 4:27)
Thine Holy One ....(Acts 2:27)
The Holy One and Just ....(Acts 3:14)
The Holy One of Israel .... (Psalm 89:18)
That Holy Thing Which Shall Be Born of Thee ....(Luke 1:35)
Holy to the Lord ....(Luke 2:23)
Our Hope .... (I Timothy 1:1)
The Hope of Glory .... (Colossians 1:27)
The Hope of His People .... (Joel 3:16)
The Hope of Israel ....(Acts 28:20)
The Hope of Their Fathers ....(Jeremiah 50:7)
The Horn of David .... (Psalm 132:17)
The Horn of the House of Israel .... (Ezekiel 29:21)
An Horn of Salvation ....(Luke 1:69)
An House of Defense .... (Psalm 31:2)
An Householder .... (Matthew 20:1)
Her Husband .... (Revelation 21:2)

I-5

I Am ....(John 18:6)
The Image of the Invisible God .... (Colossians 1:15)
Immanuel .... (Isaiah 7:14)
Innocent Blood .... (Matthew 27:4)
Isaac ....(Hebrews 11:17,18)

J-17

The Jasper Stone .... (Revelation 4:3)
Jeremiah .... (Matthew 16:14)
Jesus .... (Matthew 1:21)
Jesus Christ ....(Hebrews 13:8)
Jesus Christ the Lord ....(Romans 7:25)
Jesus Christ, the Son of God ....(John 20:31)
Jesus of Galilee .... (Matthew 26:69)
Jesus of Nazareth ....(John 1:45)
Jesus of Nazareth, the King of the Jews ....(John 19:19)
A Jew ....(John 4:9)
John the Baptist .... (Matthew 16:14)

Joseph's Son .... (Luke 4:22)
The Judge of All the Earth .... (Genesis 18:25)
The Judge of the Quick and the Dead .... (Acts 10:42)
A Judge of the Widows .... (Psalm 68:5)
The Just One .... (Acts 7:52)
This Just Person .... (Matthew 27:24)

K - 22

Thy Keeper .... (Psalm 121:5)
The Kindness and Love of God .... (Titus 3:4)
Another King .... (Acts 17:7)
The King Eternal .... (I Timothy 1:17)
The King Immortal .... (I Timothy 1:17)
The King in His Beauty .... (Isaiah 33:17)
The King Forever and Ever .... (Psalm 10:16)
The King Invisible .... (I Timothy 1:17)
The King of All the Earth .... (Psalm 47:7)
The King of Glory .... (Psalm 24:7,8)
The King of Heaven .... (Daniel 4:37)
The King of Israel .... (John 1:49)
King of Kings .... (Revelation 19:16)
The King of Peace .... (Hebrews 7:2)
The King of Righteousness .... (Hebrews 7:2)
King of Saints .... (Revelation 15:3)
The King of Salem .... (Hebrews 7:2)
The King of Terrors .... (Job 18:14)
King of the Jews .... (Matthew 2:2)
The King Who Cometh in the Name of the Lord .... (Luke 19:38)
The King's Son .... (Psalm 72:1)
The Kinsman .... (Ruth 4:14)

L-58

A Ladder .... (Genesis 28:12)
The Lamb.. (Revelation 17:14)
The Lamb of God.. (John 1:29)
The Lamb Slain from the Foundation of the World (Revelation 13:8)
The Lamb That Was Slain .... (Revelation 5:12)

The Lamb Who Is in the Midst of the Throne .... (Revelation 7:17)
The Last .... (Isaiah 44:6)
The Last Adam .... (I Corinthians 15:45)
The Lawgiver .... (James 4:12)
A Leader .... (Isaiah 55:4)
The Life.. (John 14:6)
The Lifter-Up of Mine Head .... (Psalm 3:3)
The Light .... (John 1:7)
The Light of Men .... (John 1:4)
The Light of the City .... (Revelation 21:23)
The Light of the Glorious Gospel of Christ .... (II Corinthians 4:4)
The Light of the Knowledge of the Glory of God (II Corinthians 4:6)
The Light of the Morning .... (II Samuel 23:4)
The Light of the World .... (John 8:12)
The Light of Truth .... (Psalm 43:3)
A Light to Lighten Gentiles .... (Luke 2:32)
A Light to the Gentiles .... (Isaiah 49:6)
The Lily among Thorns .... (Song of Solomon 2:2)
The Lily of the Valleys .... (Song of Solomon 2:1)
The Lion of the Tribe of Judah .... (Revelation 5:5)
The Living Bread .... (John 6:51)
The Living God .... (Psalm 42:2)
Lord - *despotes* .... (II Peter 2: 1)
Lord - *kurios* .... (John 13:13)
Lord - *rabboni* .... (Mark 10:51)
Lord Also of the Sabbath.. (Mark 2:28)
My Lord and My God .... (John 20:28)
The Lord and Savior .... (II Peter 1:11)
Lord Both of the Dead and Living .... (Romans 14:9)
The Lord from Heaven .... (I Corinthians 15:47)
Lord God Almighty .... (Revelation 16:7)
The Lord God of the Holy Prophets .... (Revelation 22:6)
Lord God of Israel .... (Psalm 41:13)
Lord God of Truth .... (Psalm 31:5)
Lord God Omnipotent .... (Revelation 19:6)
The Lord God Who Judgeth Her .... (Revelation 18:8)
The Lord, Holy and True .... (Revelation 6:10)

Lord Jesus ....(Romans 10:9)
Lord Jesus Christ .... (James 2:1)
The Lord Mighty in Battle .... (Psalm 24:8)
The Lord of All the Earth ....(Joshua 3:11)
The Lord of Glory .... (I Corinthians 2:8)
The Lord of the Harvest .... (Matthew 9:38)
The Lord of Hosts .... (Psalm 24:10)
O LORD Our Lord .... (Psalm 8:1,9)
Lord of Lords .... (I Timothy 6:15)
Lord of Peace .... (II Thessalonians 3:16)
The Lord of the Vineyard .... (Matthew 20:8)
The Lord of the Whole Earth .... (Psalm 97:5)
The Lord's Christ .... (Revelation 11:15)
The Lord's Doing .... (Matthew 21:42)
The Lord Strong and Mighty .... (Psalm 24:8)
Lowly in Heart .... (Matthew 11:29)

M - 42

Magnified (Psalm 40:16) Our Maker .... (Psalm 95:6)
A Malefactor (John 18:30) The Man ....(John 19:5)
A Man Approved of God ....(Acts 2:22)
A Man Child .... (Revelation 12:5)
The Man Christ Jesus .... (I Timothy 2:5)
A Man Gluttonous .... (Matthew 11:19)
The Man Whose Name Is the Branch ....(Zechariah 6:12)
The Man of Sorrows .... (Isaiah 53:3)
The Man Whom He Hath Ordained ....(Acts 17:31)
Manna ....(Exodus 16:15)
Marvelous in Our Eyes .... (Matthew 21:42)
The Master - *didaskalos* ....(John 1.1:28)
Master - *epistates* ....(Luke 5:5)
Your Master - *kathegetes* .... (Matthew 23:10)
The Master of the House - *oikodespotes* ....(Luke 13:25)
Master - *rabbi* ....(John 4:31)
The Meat Offering ....(Leviticus 2:1)
The Mediator .... (I Timothy 2:5)
The Mediator of a Better Covenant ....(Hebrews 8:6)

The Mediator of the New Covenant ....(Hebrews 12:24)
The Mediator of the New Testament ....(Hebrews 9:15)
Meek .... (Matthew 11:29)
Melchizedek .... (Genesis 14:18)
A Merciful and Faithful High Priest ....(Hebrews 2:17)
His Mercy and His Truth .... (Psalm 57:3)
Mercyseat ....(Hebrews 9:5; I John 2:2)
The Messenger of the Covenant ....(Malachi 3:1)
Messiah ....(Daniel 9:26)
Messiah the Prince ....(Daniel 9:25)
Mighty .... (Psalm 89:19)
The Mighty God .... (Isaiah 9:6)
The Mighty One of Jacob .... (Isaiah 49:26; 60:16)
The Minister of Sin ....(Galatians 2:17)
A Minister of the Circumcision ....(Romans 15:8)
The Minister of the Heavenly Sanctuary .... (Hebrews 8:1-3)
A More Excellent Name ....(Hebrews 1:4)
The Morning Star ....(Revelation 2:28)
The Most High .... (Psalm 9:2; 21:7)
The Mouth of God .... (Matthew 4:4)
The Mystery of God ....(Colossians 2:2)

N-5

A Nail Fastened in a Sure Place .... (Isaiah 22:23)
A Name above Every Name ....(Philippians 2:9)
A Nazarene .... (Matthew 2:23)
Thy New Name ....(Revelation 3:12)
A Nourisher of Thine Old Age .... (Ruth 4:15)

O-9

An Offering and a Sacrifice to God ....(Ephesians 5:2)
The Offspring of David ....(Revelation 22:16)
Ointment Poured Forth .... (Song of Solomon 1:3)
The Omega ....(Revelation 22:13)
His Only Begotten Son ....(John 3:16)
The Only Begotten of the Father ....(John 1:14)
Only Potentate .... (I Timothy 6:15)

The Only Wise God .... (I Timothy 1:17)
An Owl of the Desert .... (Psalm 102:6)

P - 40

Our Passover .... (I Corinthians 5:7)
The Path of Life .... (Psalm 16:11)
A Pavilion .... (Psalm 31:20)
Our Peace .... (Ephesians 2:14)
The Peace-Offering .... (Leviticus 3:1)
A Pelican of the Wilderness .... (Psalm 102:6)
A Perfect Man .... (James 3:2)
The Person of Christ .... (II Corinthians 2:10)
Physician .... (Luke 4:23)
The Pillar of Fire .... (Exodus 13:21,22)
The Place of Our Sanctuary .... (Jeremiah 17:12)
A Place of Refuge .... (Isaiah 4:6)
A Plant of Renown .... (Ezekiel 34:29)
A Polished Staff .... (Isaiah 49:2)
Poor .... (II Corinthians 8:9)
My Portion .... (Psalm 119:57)
The Portion\ of Jacob .... (Jeremiah 51:19)
The Portion of Mine Inheritance .... (Psalm 16:5)
The Potter .... (Jeremiah 18:6)
The Power of God .... (I Corinthians 1:24)
Precious .... (I Peter 2:7)
A Precious Cornerstone .... (Isaiah 28:16)
The Preeminence .... (Colossians 1:18)
A Price .... (I Corinthians 6:20)
The Price of His Redemption .... (Leviticus 25:52)
A Priest Forever .... (Psalm 110:4)
The Priest of the Most High God .... (Hebrews 7: 1)
A Prince and Savior .... (Acts 5:3 1)
The Prince of Life .... (Acts 3:15)
The Prince of Peace (Isaiah 9:6) Prince of Princes .... (Daniel 8:25)
The Prince of the Kings of the Earth .... (Revelation 1:5)
The Prophet .... (John 7:40)
A Prophet Mighty in Deed and Word .... (Luke 24:19)

The Prophet of Nazareth .... (Matthew 21:11)
A Prophet without Honor .... (Matthew 13:57)
One of the Prophets .... (Matthew 16:14)
The Propitiation for Your Sins ....(I John 2:2)
Pure ....(I John 3:3)
A Purifier of Silver .... (Malachi 3:3)

Q-2

Of Quick Understanding .... (Isaiah 11:3)
A Quickening Spirit .... (I Corinthians 15:45)

R-53

Rabbi .... (John 3:2)
Rabboni ....(John 20:16)
Rain upon the Mown Grass .... (Psalm 72:6)
A Ransom for All .... (I Timothy 2:6)
A Ransom for Many .... (Matthew 20:28)
The Red Heifer without Spot .... (Numbers 19:2)
My Redeemer ....(Job 19:25)
Redemption ....(I Corinthians 1:30; Luke 21:28)
The Redemption of Their Soul .... (Psalm 49:8)
A Refiner's Fire ....(Malachi 3:2)
Our Refuge .... (Psalm 46:1)
A Refuge in Times of Trouble .... (Psalm 9:9)
A Refuge for the Oppressed .... (Psalm 9:9)
A Refuge from the Storm .... (Isaiah 25:4)
Our Report .... (Isaiah 53:1)
A Reproach of Men .... (Psalm 22:6)
Their Resting Place ....(Jeremiah 50:6)
A Restorer of Thy Life .... (Ruth 4:15)
The Resurrection and the Life ....(John 11:25)
The Revelation of Jesus Christ .... (Revelation 1:1)
Reverend .... (Psalm 111:9)
A Reward for the Righteous .... (Psalm 58:11)
Rich ....(Romans 10:12)
The Riches of His Glory ....(Romans 9:23)
The Riddle .... (Judges 14:14)

Right ....(Deuteronomy 32:4)

The Righteous ....(I John 2: 1)

A Righteous Branch ....(Jeremiah 23:5)

The Righteous God .... (Psalm 7:9)

The Righteous Lord .... (Psalm 11:7)

My Righteous Servant .... (Isaiah 53:11)

The Righteous Judge .... (II Timothy 4:8)

A Righteous Man ....(Luke 23:47)

Righteousness .... (I Corinthians 1:30)

The Righteousness of God ....(Romans 10:3)

A River of Water in a Dry Place .... (Isaiah. 32:2)

The Rock .... (Matthew 16:18)

The Rock that Is Higher Than I .... (Psalm 61:2)

The Rock of Israel .... (II Samuel 23:3)

A Rock of Offense ....(Romans 9:33)

The Rock of My Refuge .... (Psalm 94:22)

The Rock of His Salvation.....................(Deuteronomy 32:15)

The Rock of Our Salvation .... (Psalm 95:1)

The Rock of Thy Strength .... (Isaiah 17:10)

The Rod .... (Micah 6:9)

A Rod out of the Stem of Jesse .... (Isaiah 11:1)

The Root of David .... (Revelation 5:5)

A Root of Jesse ....(Romans 15:12; Isaiah 11:10)

A Root out of Dry Ground .... (Isaiah 53:2)

The Root and Offspring of David .... (Revelation 22:16)

The Rose of Sharon .... (Song of Solomon 2:1)

A Ruler .... (Micah 5:2)

S -94

The Sacrifice for Sins ....(Hebrews 10:12)

A Sacrifice to God .... (Ephesians 5:2)

My Salvation .... (Psalm 27:1)

The Salvation of God ....(Luke 2:30; 3:6)

The Salvation of Israel ....(Jeremiah 3:23)

A Samaritan ....(John 8:48)

The Same Yesterday, Today and Forever ....(Hebrews 13:8)

A Sanctuary .... (Isaiah 8:14)

A Sardius Stone .... (Revelation 4:3)
The Saving Strength of His Anointed .... (Psalm 28:8)
Savior .... (Titus 2:13)
The Savior of All Men .... (I Timothy 4:10)
The Savior of the Body .... (Ephesians 5:23)
The Savior of the World .... (John 4:42; I John 4:14)
The Scapegoat .... (Leviticus 16:8; John 11:49-52)
The Scepter of Israel .... (Numbers 24:17)
The Scepter of Thy Kingdom .... (Psalm 45:6)
The Second Man .... (I Corinthians 15:45)
Secret .... (Judges 13:18)
The Secret of Thy Presence .... (Psalm 31:20)
The Seed of Abraham .... (Galatians 3:16)
The Seed of David .... (Romans 1:3; II Timothy 2:8)
The Seed of the Woman .... (Genesis 3:15)
The Sent One .... (John 9:4)
Separate from His Brethren .... (Genesis 49:26)
Separate from Sinners .... (Hebrews 7:26)
The Serpent in the Wilderness .... (John 3:14)
My Servant .... (Isaiah 42:1)
A Servant of Rulers .... (Isaiah 49:7)
My Servant the Branch .... (Zechariah 3:8)
A Shadow from the Heat .... (Isaiah 25:4)
The Shadow of the Almighty .... (Psalm 91:1)
The Shadow of A Great Rock .... (Isaiah 32:2)
A Shelter .... (Psalm 61:3)
My Shepherd .... (Psalm 23: 1; Isaiah 40:11)
Shepherd of Israel .... (Psalm 80:1)
Our Shield .... (Psalm 84:9)
Shiloh .... (Genesis 49:10)
Shoshannim .... (Psalm 45:Title; 69:Title)
A Sign of the Lord .... (Isaiah 7:11)
Siloam .... (John 9:7)
Sin .... (II Corinthians 5:21)
A Snare to the Inhabitants of Jerusalem .... (Isaiah 8:14)
The Son .... (Matthew 11:27)
His Son from Heaven .... (I Thessalonians 1:10)

A Son Given .... (Isaiah 9:6)

The Son of Abraham .... (Matthew 1:1)

The Son of David .... (Matthew 1:1)

The Son of God ....(John 1:49)

The Son of Joseph ....(John 1:45)

The Son of Man ....(John 1:51)

The Son of Mary ....(Mark 6:3)

The Son of the Blessed ....(Mark 14:61)

The Son of the Father .... (II John 3)

The Son of the Freewoman ....(Galatians 4:30)

The Son of the Highest ....(Luke 1:32)

The Son of the Living God .... (Matthew 16:16)

The Son of the Most High .... (Mark 5:7)

A Son over His Own House ....(Hebrews 3:6)

The Son Who Is Consecrated for Evermore ....(Hebrews 7:28)

My Song .... (Isaiah, 12:2)

A Sower .... (Matthew 13:4,37)

A Sparrow Alone upon the Housetop ....(Psalm 102:7)

That Spiritual Rock .... (I Corinthians 10:4)

A Star out of Jacob ....(Numbers 24:17)

My Stay .... (Psalm 18:18)

A Stone Cut out of the Mountain ....(Daniel 2:45)

A Stone Cut without Hands ....(Daniel 2:34)

The Stone of Israel .... (Genesis 49:24)

A Stone of Stumbling .... (I Peter 2:8)

The Stone Which the Builders Refused ....(Psalm 118:22)

The Stone Which the Builders Rejected .... (Matthew 21:42)

The Stone Which Was Set at Nought ....(Acts 4:11)

A Stranger .... (Matthew 25:35)

My Strength .... (Isaiah 12:2)

The Strength of Israel ....(I Samuel 15:29)

The Strength of My Life .... (Psalm 27:1)

A Strength to the Needy in Distress .... (Isaiah 25:4)

A Strength to the Poor .... (Isaiah 25:4)

Strong .... (Psalm 24:8)

A Strong Consolation ....(Hebrews 6:18)

A Stronghold in the Day of Trouble .... (Nahum 1:7)

141

A Strong Lord .... (Psalm 89:8)
My Strong Refuge .... (Psalm 71:7)
My Strong Rock .... (Psalm 31:2)
A Strong Tower .... (Proverbs 18:10)
A Strong Tower from the Enemy .... (Psalm 61:3)
A Stronger than He ....(Luke 11:22)
A Stumbling Block .... (I Corinthians 1:23)
The Sun of Righteousness ....(Malachi 4:2)
A Sure Foundation .... (Isaiah 28:16)
The Sure Mercies of David .... (Isaiah 55:3; Acts 13:34)
A Surety of A Better Testament ....(Hebrews 7:22)
A Sweet-Smelling Savor .... (Ephesians 5:2)

T-19

A Tabernacle for a Shadow .... (Isaiah 4:6)
The Tabernacle of God .... (Revelation 21:3)
Teacher .... (Matthew 10:25)
A Teacher Come from God .... (John 3:2)
The Temple .... (John 2:19)
The Tender Grass .... (II Samuel 23:4)
A Tender Plant .... (Isaiah 53:2)
The Tender Mercy of God .... (Luke 1:78)
The Testator ....(Hebrews 9:16,17)
The Testimony of God .... (I Corinthians 2:1)
This Treasure .... (II Corinthians 4:7)
The Trespass Offering ....(Leviticus 5:6)
A Tried Stone .... (Isaiah 28:16)
The True Bread from Heaven ....(John 6:32)
The True God ....(Jeremiah 10:10)
The True Light .... (John 1:9)
The True Vine .... (John 15:1)
The True Witness .... (Proverbs 14:25)
The Truth ....(John 14:6)

U-7

Undefiled ....(Hebrews 7:26)
Understanding .... (Proverbs 3:19)

The Unknown God ....(Acts 17:23)
The Unspeakable Gift .... (II Corinthians 9:15)
The Urim and Thummin .... (Exodus 28:30)
The Upholder of All Things ....(Hebrews 1:3)
Upright .... (Psalm 92:15)

V-7

The Veil ....(Hebrews 10:20)
The Very God of Peace .... (I Thessalonians 5:23)
Very Great .... (Psalm 104:1)
A Very Present Help in Trouble .... (Psalm 46:1)
The Victory .... (I Corinthians 15:54)
The Vine ....(John 15:5)
The Voice .... (Revelation 1:12)

W - 24

A Wall of Fire .... (Zechariah 2:5)
The Wave-Offering ....(Leviticus 7:30)
The Way ....(John 14:6)
The Way of Holiness .... (Isaiah 35:8)
The Weakness of God .... (I Corinthians 1:25)
A Wedding Garment .... (Matthew 22:12)
The Well of Living Waters ....(John 4:14)
The Well of Salvation .... (Isaiah 12:3)
Wisdom .... (I Corinthians 1:25)
The Wisdom of God .... (I Corinthians 1:24)
A Wise Master Builder .... (I Corinthians 3:10)
Witness .... (Judges 11:10)
My Witness .... (Job 16:19)
The Witness of God ....(I John 5:9)
A Witness to the People .... (Isaiah 55:4)
Wonderful .... (Judges 13:18)
Wonderful Counselor .... (Isaiah 9:6)
The Word ....(John 1:1)
The Word of God .... (Revelation 19:13)
The Word of Life ....(I John 1:1)
A Worm and No Man .... (Psalm 22:6)

Worthy .... (Revelation 4:11; 5:12)
That Worthy Name .... (James 2:7)
Worthy to be Praised .... (Psalm 18:3)

X-2

X as Chi The Traditional Symbol of Christ
X as an Unknown Quantity .... (Revelation 19:12)

Y-2

The Yokefellow .... (Matthew 11:29-30)
The Young Child .... (Matthew 2:11)

Z-4

Zaphnath-paaneah .... (Genesis 41:45)
The Zeal of the Lord of Hosts .... (Isaiah 37:32)
The Zeal of Thine House ....(John 2:17; Psalm 69:9)
Zerubbabel ....(Zechariah 4:7,9)

Total Names and Titles - 675

MY PREEMINENT
PRONOUNS IN SCRIPTURE

Who Art, and Wast, and Shalt Be .... (Revelation 16:5)
Him That Bringeth Good Tidings ....(Nahum 1:15)
He Who Brought Us Up .... (Joshua 24:17)
He Who Created .... (Revelation 10:6)
He That Cometh... (Luke 7:19; Matthew 11:14)
He That Cometh after Me .... (John 1:15, 27)
He Who Cometh down from Heaven .... (John 6:33)
He That Cometh in the Name of the Lord ....(Matthew 21:9)
He That Cometh into the World .... (John 11:27)
Who Coverest Thyself with Light ....(Psalm 104:2)
Who Crowneth Thee with Loving-Kindness ....(Psalm 103:4)
He That was Dead and Is Alive .... (Revelation 2:8)

Who Dwelleth in Zion ....(Psalm 9:11)
He Who Fighteth for You .... (Joshua 23:10)
He That Filleth All in All .... (Ephesians 1:23)
Who Forgiveth All Thine Iniquities ....(Psalm 103:3)
This That Forgiveth Sins .... (Luke 7:49)
Who Girdeth Me with Strength ....(Psalm 18:32)
Who Giveth Me Counsel ....(Psalm 16:7)
He That Hath the Bride .... (John 3:29)
He Who Hath His Eyes Like a Flame of Fire .... (Revelation 2:18)
He Who Hath His Feet Like Fine Brass .... (Revelation 2:18)
Thou Who Hearest Prayer ....(Psalm 65:2)
Who Healeth all Thy Diseases ....(Psalm 103:3)
He That Is Higher Than the Highest .... (Ecclesiastes 5:8)
He That Holdeth the Seven Stars .... (Revelation 2:1)
He That Is Holy .... (Revelation 3:7)
He That Keepeth Israel ....(Psalm 121:4)
He That Hath the Key of David .... (Revelation 3:7)
Who Laid the Foundations of the Earth ....(Psalm 104:5)
Who Layeth the Beams of His Chambers in the Waters (Psalm 104:3)
Thou Who Liftest Me up from the Gates of Death ....(Psalm 9:13)
He That Liveth .... (Revelation 1:18)
Him That Liveth Forever and Ever .... (Revelation 10:6)
Him That Loveth Us .... (Revelation 1:5)
Who Maketh His Angels Spirits .... (Psalm 104:4; Hebrews 1:7)
Who Maketh the Clouds His Chariot ....(Psalm 104:3)
He That Openeth .... (Revelation 3:7)
Who Hast Power over These Plagues .... (Revelation 16:9)
Who Redeemeth Thy Life from Destruction ....(Psalm 103:4)
Thou Rulest the Raging of the Sea ....(Psalm 89:9)
He That Sanctifieth .... (Hebrews 2:11)
Who Satisfieth Thy Mouth with Good Things ....(Psalm 103:5)
Thou Who Saveth by Thy Right Hand ....(Psalm 17:7)
Who Saveth the Upright in Heart ....(Psalm 7:10)
He Who Searcheth .... (Revelation 2:23)
Whom Thou hast Sent .... (John 17:3)
He Who Hath the Seven Spirits of God .... (Revelation 3:1)
He Who Hath the Sharp Sword with Two Edges .... (Revelation 2:12)

He that Shutteth .... (Revelation 3:7)
He Who Sitteth in the Heavens .... (Psalm 2:4)
Him That Sitteth on the Throne .... (Revelation 6:16)
Who Stretchest out the Heavens Like a Curtain ....(Psalm 104:2)
He Who Testifieth .... (Revelation 22:20)
He That Is True .... (Revelation 3:7)
Him That Was Valued ....(Matthew 27:9)
He Who Walks in the Midst of the Seven Candlesticks (Revelation 2: 1)
He Who Walketh upon the Wings of the Wind ....(Psalm 104:3)

Total - 58

COMPOUND NAMES OF THE LORD GOD (JEHOVAH EL) IN SCRIPTURE

El Elohim Jehovah - The Lord God of gods .... (Joshua 22:22)
Jehovah Elohim - The Lord God ....(Genesis 2:4; 3:9-13,21)
Jehovah Elohe 'Abothekem -
    The Lord God of Your Fathers .... (Joshua 18:3)
Jehovah El Elyon - The Lord, the Most High God ......(Genesis 14:22)
Jehovah El 'Emeth - The Lord God of Truth ....(Psalm 31:5)
Jehovah El Gemuwal -
    The Lord God of Recompense .... (Jeremiah 51:56)
Jehovah Elohim Tseba'oth - The Lord God of Hosts ....(Psalm 59:5)
Jehovah Elohe Yeshu athi -
    The Lord God of my Salvation ....(Psalm 88:1)
Jehovah Elohe Yisra'el - The Lord God of Israel ....(Psalm 41:13)

Total - 9

NAMES OF GOD (ELOHIM) IN SCRIPTURE

Elohim - God ....(Genesis 1:1)
Elohim Bashamayim - God in Heaven .... (Joshua 2:11)

El Bethel - The God of the House of God ....(Genesis 35:7)
Elohe Chaseddiy - God of My Mercy ....(Psalm 59:10)
El Elohe Yisra'el -
    God, the God of Israel ....(Genesis 33:20; Psalm 68:8)
El Elyon - The Most High God ....(Genesis 14:18)
El Emunah - A Faithful God ....(Deuteronomy 7:9)
El Gibbor - The Mighty God ....(Isaiah 9:6)
El Hakabodh - The God of Glory ....(Psalm 29:3)
El Hayyay - God of My Life ....(Psalm 42:8)
El He - The Living God .... (Joshua 3:10)
El Kana - A Jealous God .... (Exodus 20:5)
Elohim Kedoshim - A Holy God .... (Joshua 24:19)
El Kenno' - A Jealous God .... (Joshua 24:19)
Elohe Ma'ozi - God of My Strength ....(Psalm 43:2)
Elohim Machaseh Lanu - God Our Refuge ....(Psalm 62:8)
Eli Malekhi - God My King ....(Psalm 68:24)
El Marom - God Most High ....(Psalm 57:2)
El Nakamoth - God that Avengeth ....(Psalm 18:47)
El Nose' - God that Forgave ....(Psalm 99:8)
Elohenu 'Olam - The Everlasting God ....(Psalm 48:14)
Elohim 'Ozer Li - God My Helper ....(Psalm 54:4)
El Ra'i - Thou God Seest Me ....(Genesis 16:13)
El Sela - God, My Rock ....(Psalm 42:9)
El Shaddai - The Almighty God ....(Genesis 17:1,2)
Elohim Shephtim Ba arets -
    God that Judgeth in the Earth ....(Psalm 58:11)
El Simchath Gili - God My Exceeding Joy ....(Psalm 43:4)
Elohim Tseba'oth - God of Hosts ....(Psalm 80:7)
Elohe Tishu'athi - God of my Salvation ....(Psalm 18:46; 51:14)
Elohe Tsadeki - God of my Righteousness ....(Psalm 4:1)
Elohe Ya'akob - God of Jacob ....(Psalm 20:1; 46:7)
Elohe Yisra'el - God of Israel ....(Psalm 59:5)

Total - 32

NAMES OF JEHOVAH
IN SCRIPTURE

Jehovah - The Lord .... (Exodus 6:2,3)
Adonai Jehovah - The Lord God ....(Genesis 15:2)
Jehovah Adon Kal Ha arets -
  The Lord, the Lord of All the Earth .... (Joshua 3:13)
Jehovah Bara - The Lord Creator ....(Isaiah 40:28)
Jehovah Chatsahi - The Lord My Strength ....(Psalm 27:1)
Jehovah Chereb - The Lord . . . the Sword ....(Deuteronomy 33:29)
Jehovah Eli - The Lord My God ....(Psalm 18:2)
Jehovah Elyon - The Lord Most High ....(Psalm 38:2)
Jehovah 'Ez Lami - The Lord My Strength ....(Psalm 28:7)
Jehovah Gador Milchaniah -
  The Lord Mighty in Battle ....(Psalm 24:8)
Jehovah Ganan - The Lord Our Defence ....(Psalm 89:18)
Jehovah Go'el - The Lord Thy Redeemer (Isaiah 49:26; 60:16) *Jehovah Hashopet* - The Lord the Judge ....(Judges 6:27)
Jehovah Hoshe'ah - The Lord Save ....(Psalm 20:9)
Jehovah 'Immeku - The Lord Is with you ....(Judges 6:12)
Jehovah 'Izoz Hakaboth -
  The Lord Strong and Mighty ....(Psalm 24:8)
Jehovah Jireh - The Lord Will Provide ....(Genesis 22:14)
Jehovah Kabodhi - The Lord My Glory ....(Psalm 3:3)
Jehovah Kanna -
  The Lord Whose Name Is Jealous .... (Exodus 34:14)
Jehovah Keren-Yish'i -
  The Lord the Horn of My Salvation ....(Psalm 18:2)
Jehovah Machsi - The Lord My Refuge ....(Psalm 91:9)
Jehovah Magen - The Lord, the Shield ....(Deuteronomy 33:29)
Jehovah Ma'oz - The Lord ... My Fortress ....(Jeremiah 16:19)
Hamelech Jehovah - The Lord the King ....(Psalm 98:6)
Jehovah Melech 'Olam - The Lord King Forever ....(Psalm 10:16)
Jehovah Mephald - The Lord My Deliverer ....(Psalm 18:2)
Jehovah M'gaddishcem - The Lord Our Sanctifier....... (Exodus 31:13)
Jehovah Metsodhathi - The Lord ... My Fortress ....(Psalm 18:2)

Jehovah Misqabbi - The Lord My High Tower ....(Psalm 18:2)
Jehovah Naheh - The Lord that Smiteth ....(Ezekiel 7:9)
Jehovah Nissi - The Lord Our Banner .... (Exodus 17:15)
Jehovah 'Ori - The Lord My Light ....(Psalm 27:1)
Jehovah Rapha - The Lord that Healeth .... (Exodus 15:26)
Jehovah Rohi - The Lord My Shepherd ....(Psalm 23: 1)
Jehovah Sabaoth - The Lord of Hosts .... (I Samuel 1:3)
Jehovah Sel'i - The Lord My Rock ....(Psalm 18:2)
Jehovah Shalom - The Lord Our Peace ....(Judges 6:24)
Jehovah Shammah - The Lord Is There ....(Ezekiel 48:35)
Jehovah Tiskenu - The Lord Our Righteousness .... (Jeremiah 23:6)
Jehovah Tsori - O Lord My Strength ....(Psalm 19:14)
Jehovah 'Uzam - The Lord Their Strength ....(Psalm 37:39)
Jehovah Yasha - The Lord Thy Savior .... (Isaiah 49:26; 60:16
Total – 42

A SELECTED BIBLIOGRAPHY OF MY NAMES

Hahn, Ferdinand. *The Titles of Jesus in Christology: Their History in Early Christianity.*

Tr. Harold Knight and George Ogg. Cleveland, Ohio: The World Publishing Company, 1969.

Hausherr, Irenee. *The Name of Jesus.* Tr. Charles Cummings. Kalamazoo, Michigan: Cistercian Publications Inc., 1978.

Hill, Rowley. *52 Sermon Outlines on the Titles of Our Lord.* Grand Rapids, Michigan: Baker Book House, 1958.

Horton, T. C. and Hurlbut, Charles E. *The Wonderful Names of Our Wonderful Lord.* Los Angeles: Grant Publishing House, 1925.

Keller, W. Phillip. *A Layman Looks at the Lamb of God.* Minneapolis, Minnesota: Bethany House Publishers, 1982.

Krumwiede, Walter. *Names of Jesus: A Practical and Devotional Study of Some of the Names of Jesus.* Philadelphia: The United Lutheran Publication House, 1927.

Large, James. *Two Hundred and Eighty Titles and Symbols of Christ.* Grand Rapids, Michigan: Baker Book House, 1959.

Lee, Robert. *Similies of Our Lord and "His Own" or Bible Word Pictures of our Lord and of the Christian.* London: Pickering & Inglis, n.d.

Lockyer, Herbert. "The Greatest of All Bible Men, Jesus Christ," in *All the Men of the Bible.* Grand Rapids, Michigan: Zondervan Publishing House, 1958.

Rolls, Charles J. *The Indescribable Christ: The Names and Titles of Jesus Christ.* Grand Rapids, Michigan: Zondervan Publishing House, 1953.

Rolls, Charles J. *The World's Greatest Name: The Names and Titles of Jesus Christ.* Grand Rapids, Michigan: Zondervan Publishing House, 1956.

Rolls, Charles J. *Time's Noblest Name: The Names and Titles of Jesus Christ (L Through O).* Grand Rapids, Michigan: Zondervan Publishing House, 1958.

Rolls, Charles J. *The Name Above Every Name: The Names and Titles of Jesus Christ (P. Q. R. S.).* Neptune, New Jersey: Loizeaux Brothers, 1965.

Rolls, Charles J. *His Glorious Names: The Names and Titles of Jesus Christ (T. U. V. W.).* Neptune, New Jersey Loizeaux Brothers, 1975.

Spurgeon, Charles Haddon. *Sermons on Christ's Names and Titles.* Ed. Charles T. Cook. Grand Rapids, Michigan: Zondervan Publishing House, 1961.

Stevenson, Herbert F. *Titles of the Triune God: Studies in Divine Self-Revelation.* Westwood, New Jersey: Fleming H. Revell Company, 1956.

Taylor, Vincent. *The Names of Jesus.* London: Macmillan and Co., Limited, 1953.

Warfield, Benjamin B. *The Lord of Glory: A Study of the Designations of Our Lord in the New Testament with Especial Reference to His Deity.* Grand Rapids, Michigan: Baker Book House, 1976.

COMING FALL OF 2018

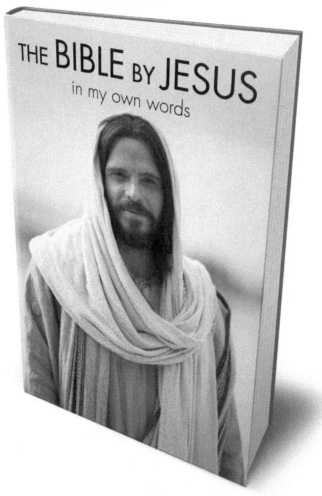

This dynamic paraphrase of the whole Bible is different from anything you've ever read before. Jesus narrates the Scriptures as only the Creator of all things could possibly share. You will see the creation, fall of man, and ultimately the restoration of all things from a vantage point never experience until now. This Bible will forever change how you read and experience the Scriptures.

ISBN 978-0-7684-1991-7   eBook: 978-0-7684-1992-4